Contents

Your HUMAN BODY workbook comes with a tray of specially chosen components to use in fun activities that have been designed to help you understand how your body works. The tray includes a set of acetate (clear plastic) sheets showing all the body's systems, 10 sticker sheets, and a magnifier.

Basic Building Blocks

Cells	2

Circulatory System

Heart	3
Circulation	4
Blood	5

Nervous System

Brain	6
Nerves	7

Respiratory System

Breathing	8
Exercising Your Lungs	9

Digestive System

Digestion	10
Enzymes	11
Mouth	12
Food	13

Excretory System

Kidneys and Bladder	14
Water	15

Endocrine System

Hormones	16

Sensory System

Seeing	17
Hearing	18
Smell	19
Taste	20
Touch	21

Reproductive System

A New Baby	22
Looking Alike	23
Growth and Development	24

Muscular System

Muscles	25
Involuntary Muscles	26

Skeletal System

Skeleton	27
Joints	28
Bones	29

Integumentary System

Skin	30
Hair and Nails	31

Answers	32
Body Facts	inside back cover

Starting Out

The Body Machine

Here are a few incredible facts about the human body: it has 206 bones, 62,500 miles of blood vessels, and 50 million million cells! Your heart pumps blood, your lungs take in oxygen, and your stomach digests food, day and night without stopping, and without you thinking about it. Your body is an amazing machine!

How to use this Book

Your HUMAN BODY workbook makes it easy to understand how your body works. It is full of essential facts, with fascinating photographs, illustrations, and diagrams, all in full color.

Each subject has a left-hand page with the key information, and a right-hand work page with activities for you to complete. The answers to the activities are shown at the end of the book, so you can check to see just how much you have learned about your body!

Your Workbook

Your workbook transforms into a self-contained worktop. Just follow these easy instructions:

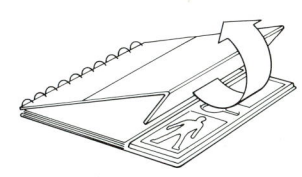

Lift up your workbook cover and fold out the inside flap.

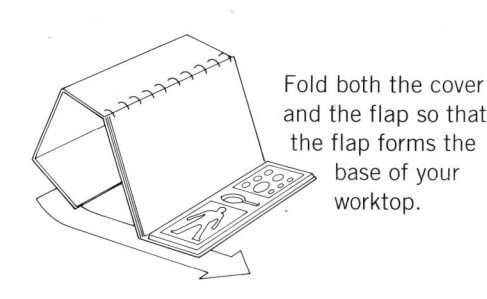

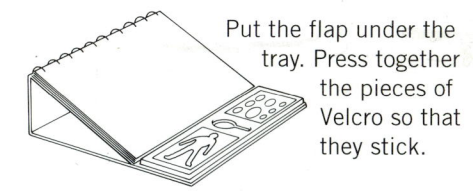

Fold both the cover and the flap so that the flap forms the base of your worktop.

Put the flap under the tray. Press together the pieces of Velcro so that they stick.

Finding the Right Pages

▶ ◀ Line up the arrows and you'll have the right subject with each activity page. You can turn them separately as well – for example, if you want to check some facts in another subject.

CELLS

Your body is made up of trillions of living units called **cells**. Each cell is so small that the period at the end of this sentence is bigger than the largest human cell, which is the egg cell in a woman.

Body Tissue
Your body has many different kinds of cell. Each one is designed for a particular job. Groups of the same sort of cell are called **tissue**. Skin, muscles, blood, and nerves are all types of body tissue.

Growing
Everyone begins life when a sperm cell from their father joins an egg cell from their mother (see page 22). New cells are being made all the time as you grow, and to replace old cells.

Inside a Cell
Though different cells do not look the same, they do have the same basic structure as the cutaway cell shown on the right.

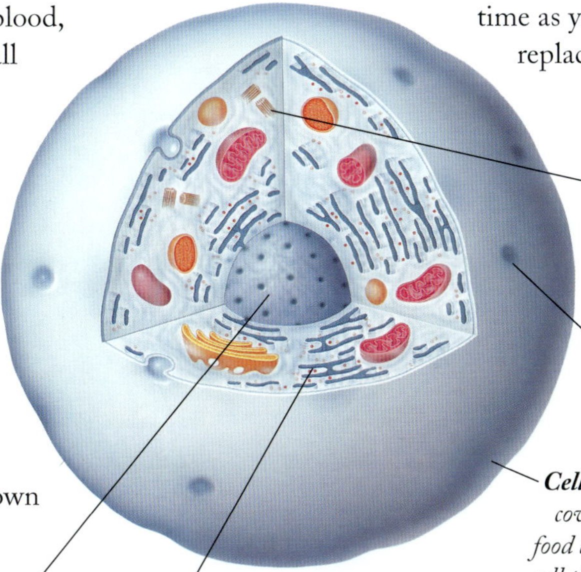

Centrioles: help enable cells to divide

Pore: an opening in the cell membrane

Cell membrane: a thin covering which allows food and oxygen into the cell through pores. It also allows waste to escape from the cell

Nucleus: the control center of the cell

Cytoplasm: a jelly-like liquid in which other parts of the cell float

Different Kinds of Cells

Egg cell: stores food for the unborn baby

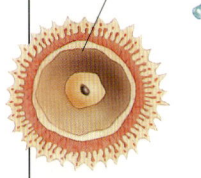

Muscle cell: will stretch and squeeze

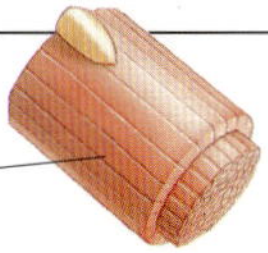

Cheek cell: protects inside of the mouth

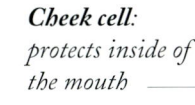

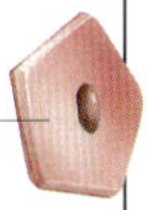

Sperm cell: moves its tail to swim to an egg cell

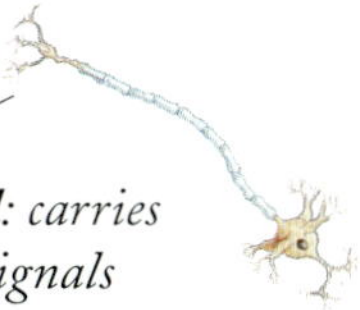

Nerve cell: carries electrical signals through the body

Intestinal cell: absorbs digested food

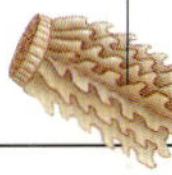

HEART

Your heart is a special set of muscles. It works all day and all night, pumping blood around your body. The blood travels in tubes called **blood vessels**.

Your heart lies inside your chest, just left of the center. Its exact position in the body is shown on the circulation acetate. Each time your heart beats, it pumps blood through your blood vessels creating a pulse. Press two fingers gently on the underside of your wrist (see top right) and feel the blood pumping through your blood vessels.

The heart is divided into four chambers. These are shown in the cutaway picture below. Blood flows to and from the heart in the order shown by the numbers next to each caption. The wall of the left ventricle is thickest because it has to pump blood around the body.

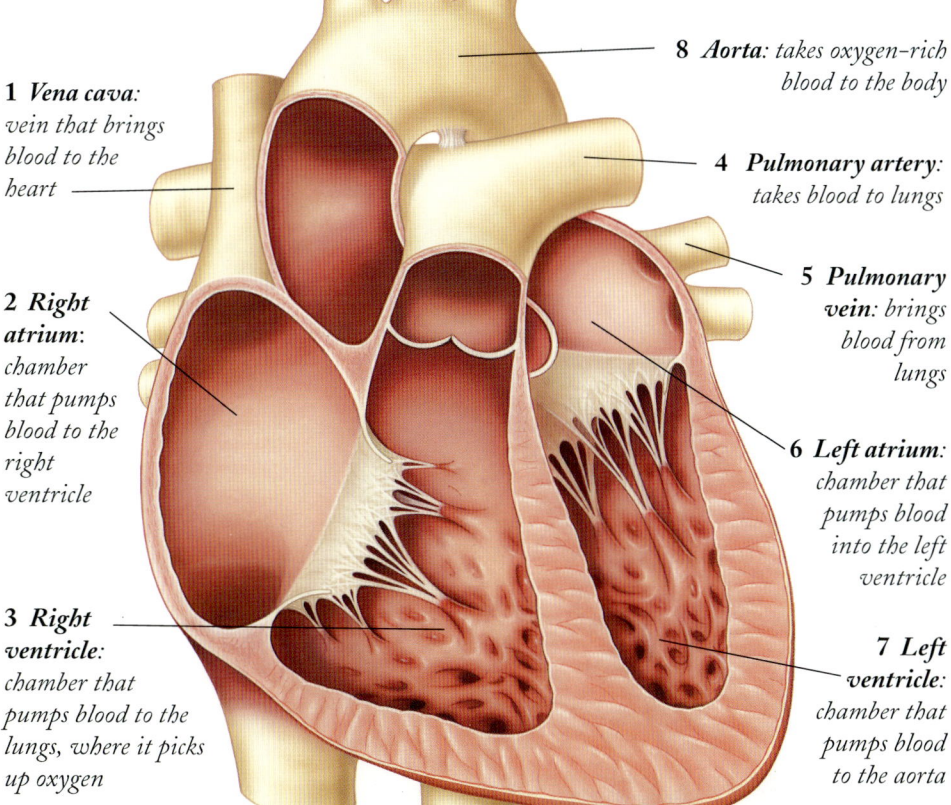

1 *Vena cava*: vein that brings blood to the heart

2 *Right atrium*: chamber that pumps blood to the right ventricle

3 *Right ventricle*: chamber that pumps blood to the lungs, where it picks up oxygen

8 *Aorta*: takes oxygen-rich blood to the body

4 *Pulmonary artery*: takes blood to lungs

5 *Pulmonary vein*: brings blood from lungs

6 *Left atrium*: chamber that pumps blood into the left ventricle

7 *Left ventricle*: chamber that pumps blood to the aorta

CIRCULATION

Your blood delivers oxygen and nutrients (foods) to your body's cells. It circulates (travels round and round) your body through a system of blood vessels. These are the highways of your body.

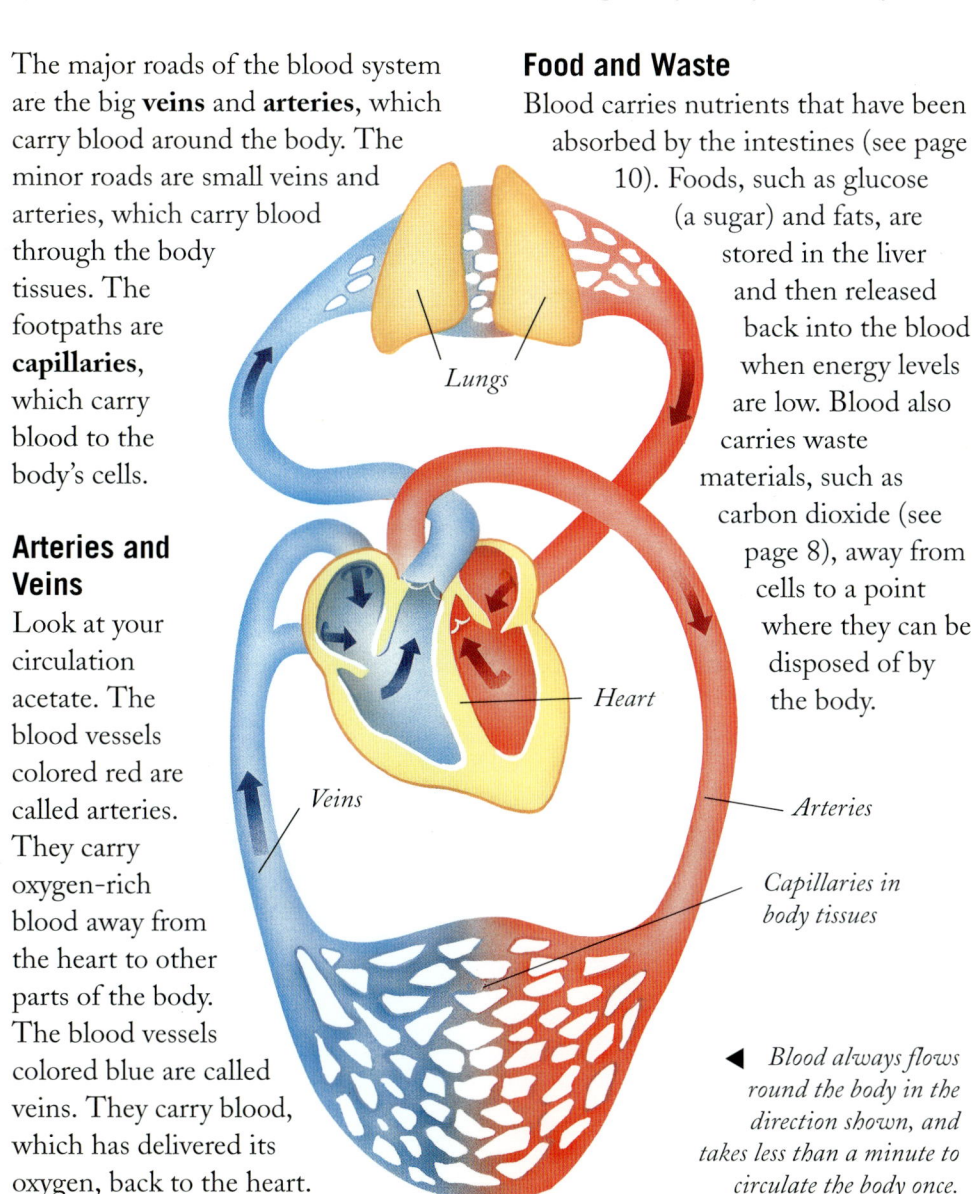

The major roads of the blood system are the big **veins** and **arteries**, which carry blood around the body. The minor roads are small veins and arteries, which carry blood through the body tissues. The footpaths are **capillaries**, which carry blood to the body's cells.

Arteries and Veins

Look at your circulation acetate. The blood vessels colored red are called arteries. They carry oxygen-rich blood away from the heart to other parts of the body. The blood vessels colored blue are called veins. They carry blood, which has delivered its oxygen, back to the heart.

Food and Waste

Blood carries nutrients that have been absorbed by the intestines (see page 10). Foods, such as glucose (a sugar) and fats, are stored in the liver and then released back into the blood when energy levels are low. Blood also carries waste materials, such as carbon dioxide (see page 8), away from cells to a point where they can be disposed of by the body.

Lungs

Heart

Veins

Arteries

Capillaries in body tissues

◀ *Blood always flows round the body in the direction shown, and takes less than a minute to circulate the body once.*

BLOOD

Blood looks like red liquid. In fact, it is made up of **red blood cells**, **white blood cells**, and **platelets**, all floating in a pale yellow, watery solution called **plasma**. Most of the cells are red blood cells which give blood its color, and carry oxygen around the body.

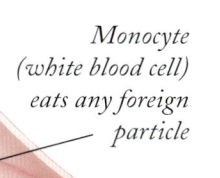

Monocyte (white blood cell) eats any foreign particle

Platelets

When you cut yourself, platelets gather around the wound and stick together to form a barrier, or blood clot. This stops you bleeding. The clot then hardens to form a scab. The scab protects the skin until the cut heals, and then it falls off.

Red blood cells

Platelets

White Blood Cells

There are many kinds of white blood cell, but they all protect the body against infection. **Lymphocytes** produce chemicals called antibodies, which wipe out bacteria and viruses. **Neutrophils** eat any invading germs.

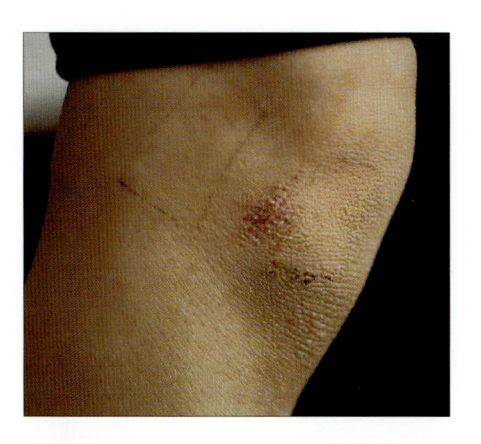

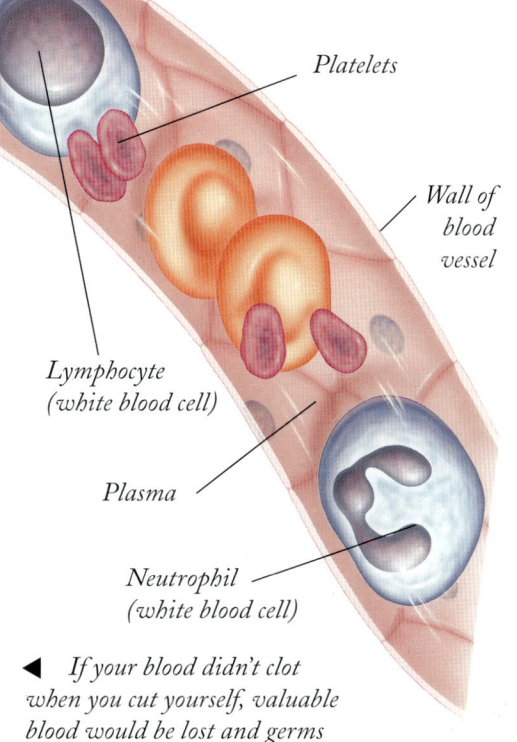

Wall of blood vessel

Lymphocyte (white blood cell)

Plasma

Neutrophil (white blood cell)

◀ *If your blood didn't clot when you cut yourself, valuable blood would be lost and germs would enter your body.*

BRAIN

Your brain is the control center of your body. It enables you to move, to think, and to sense things. Your brain needs careful protection, and floats in a shockproof fluid inside the bony armor of your skull. Locate the brain on your nervous system acetate.

▶ The things that we do are controlled by different parts of the brain. The colored areas opposite show the main control centers.

Movement and balance

Thinking

Hearing

Touch

Sight

Cerebral cortex: the outer part of the brain, also called gray matter. It contains millions of nerve cells, which receive and send out instructions to the rest of the body

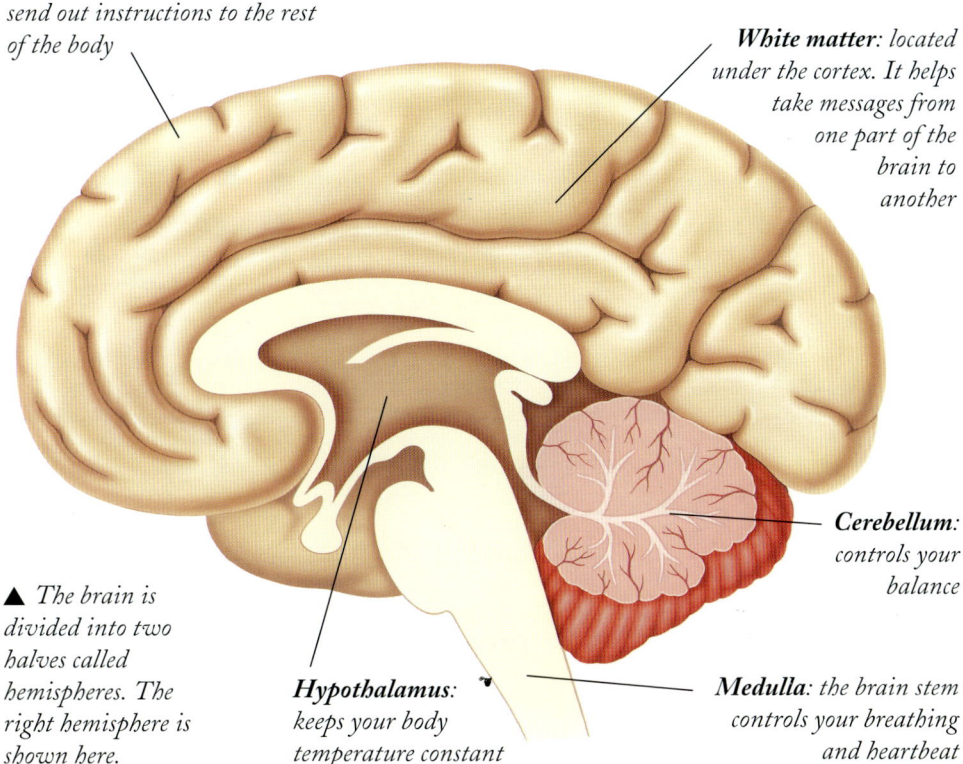

White matter: located under the cortex. It helps take messages from one part of the brain to another

Cerebellum: controls your balance

▲ The brain is divided into two halves called hemispheres. The right hemisphere is shown here.

Hypothalamus: keeps your body temperature constant

Medulla: the brain stem controls your breathing and heartbeat

NERVES

Nerves are like telephone wires. They spread out over the whole of your body and carry messages to and from the control center, your brain. Nerves carry messages around your body using tiny amounts of electricity.

The Spinal Cord
Your spinal cord is a long bundle of nerves. It runs to and from your brain down the inside of your backbone. If you look at the nervous system acetate, you'll see that long, thin nerves branch off from your spinal cord, connecting it to nearly every part of your body.

Different Nerves
Sensory nerves send messages from your skin, muscles, and organs to your brain. When your brain has decided what to do, it sends messages along **motor nerves** to your muscles, telling them how to react.

Reflex Actions
If you touch something hot or step on a pin, you will suddenly pull your hand or foot away. This is a **reflex** action. You react instantly because a warning message is sent along a sensory nerve to your spinal cord and then straight back to your muscles, before it is sent to your brain.

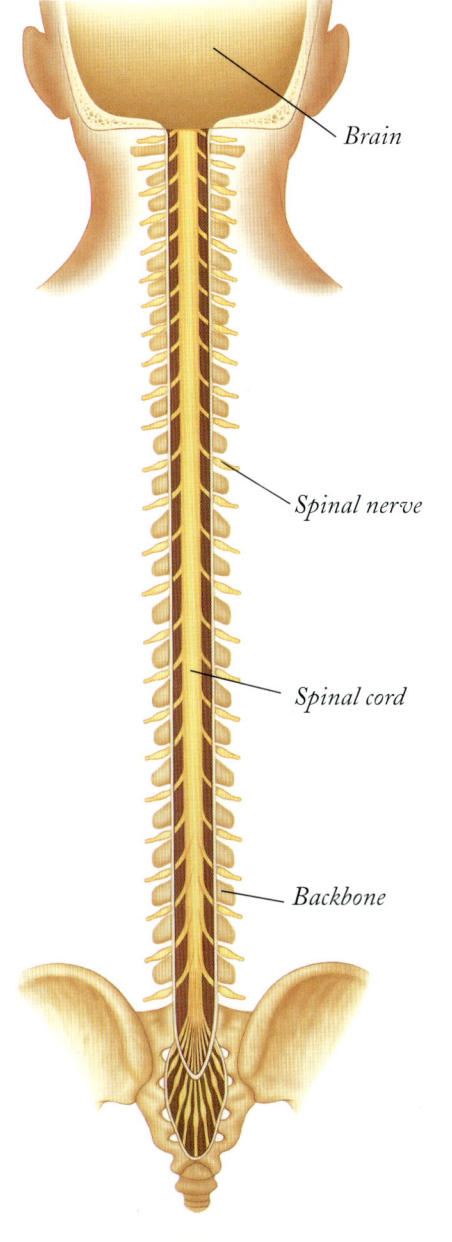

Brain

Spinal nerve

Spinal cord

Backbone

BREATHING

When you breathe, you move air in and out of your lungs. These are light and spongy because they are filled with millions of tiny air bags. The structure of a lung resembles the trunk and branches of a tree. Lungs are shown on the respiratory system acetate.

Oxygen

Oxygen is a gas in the air around you. Breathing in takes oxygen from the air into your lungs. Your body's cells (see page 2) need oxygen to burn food and release energy. This process is called **respiration**.

Breathing In

Air enters your breathing system through your nose or mouth. It then passes down your **trachea** (windpipe) and into two tubes called **bronchi**. From there the air passes through lots of increasingly narrow tubes. The smallest are called the **bronchioles**. At the end of the bronchioles are bunches of tiny sacs (bags) called **alveoli**, which fill with air. The alveoli are covered in blood capillaries, which absorb oxygen into your blood. This carries the oxygen around your body.

Breathing Out

The gas carbon dioxide, a waste product of respiration, passes from your blood into the alveoli. Then it passes through the bronchioles and bronchi, up the trachea, and out through your mouth or nose.

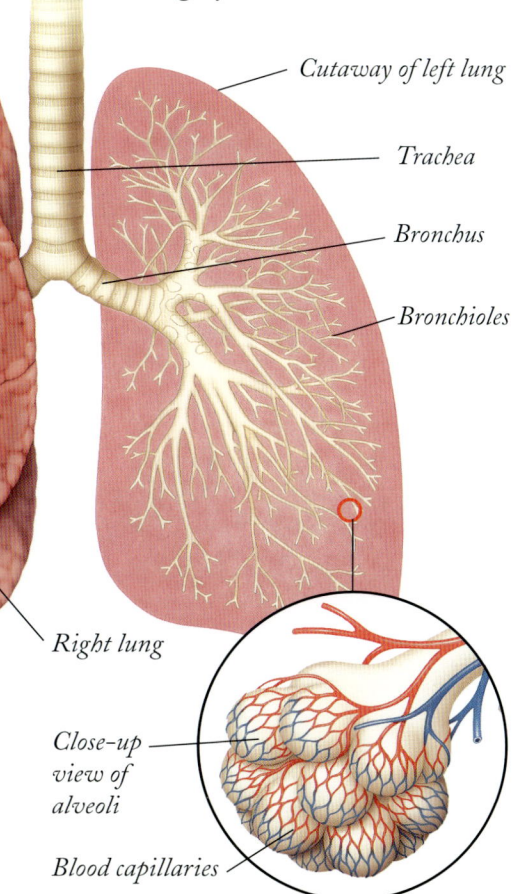

Cutaway of left lung
Trachea
Bronchus
Bronchioles
Right lung
Close-up view of alveoli
Blood capillaries

Exercising Your Lungs

Breathing is controlled by the nervous system, and happens without you thinking about it.

Breathing In and Out

To breathe in, the **diaphragm** (a strong muscle below your ribs) moves down, and your chest muscles move your rib cage up and out. Your lungs expand to fill the extra space, and suck in air. When you breathe out, your diaphragm moves up and your rib cage moves down again. This squeezes the air out of your lungs.

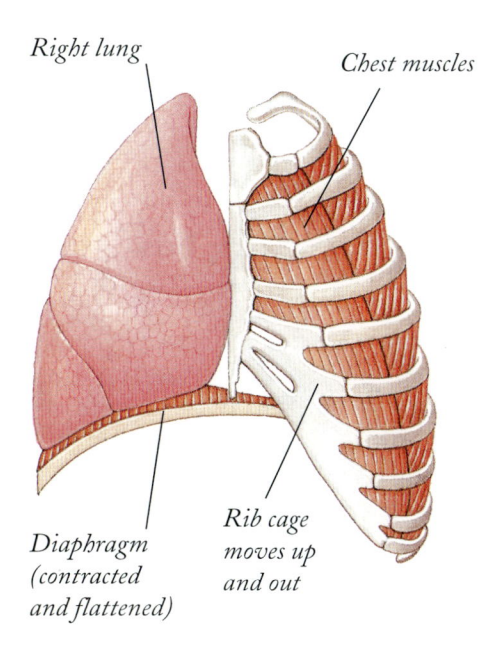

▲ *When you are active, your body needs more oxygen, so you breathe faster to take in extra air. Your heart beats faster too, to take oxygen-rich blood to your muscles quickly.*

Right lung

Chest muscles

Diaphragm (contracted and flattened)

Rib cage moves up and out

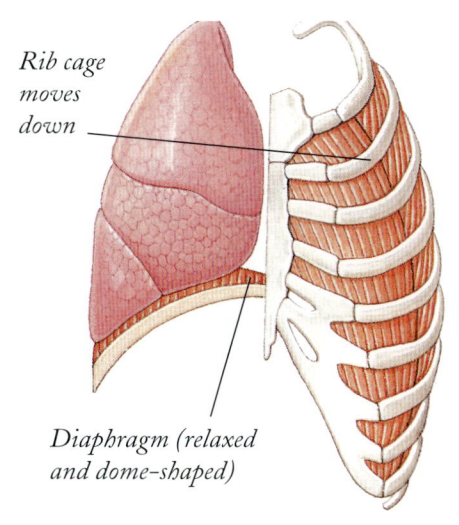

Rib cage moves down

Diaphragm (relaxed and dome-shaped)

▲ *The position of the diaphragm and ribs when you breathe in.*

▲ *The position of the diaphragm and ribs when you breathe out.*

DIGESTION

The food you eat gives you energy, keeps you warm, and enables you to grow. To absorb food, your body must first break it down into smaller and smaller pieces. This process is called **digestion**.

Digestion starts in your mouth. Your teeth grind and tear food into small pieces. The **salivary glands** squirt saliva into your mouth to make the food soft enough to swallow.

The Stomach
When you swallow food, it is pushed down a tube called the **esophagus** to the stomach. The stomach muscles churn the food and mix it with digestive juices. When the food is liquidized it passes into the **small intestine**.

Small and Large Intestine
Your intestine is a long, winding tube linking your stomach with your anus. Digestive chemicals called **enzymes** (see page 11) in your small intestine break down food until it is tiny enough to be absorbed into the blood. Food that can't be digested passes through the **large intestine** and out of the **anus**.

The Liver
Your liver stores nutrients (the useful parts of the food) and releases them into your blood when they are needed. It also makes **bile**, a green liquid, which is sent to your small intestine to help break down fats in your food. Bile is stored in your **gallbladder**. Your **pancreas** (see page 16) also makes digestive juices which flow into your small intestine.

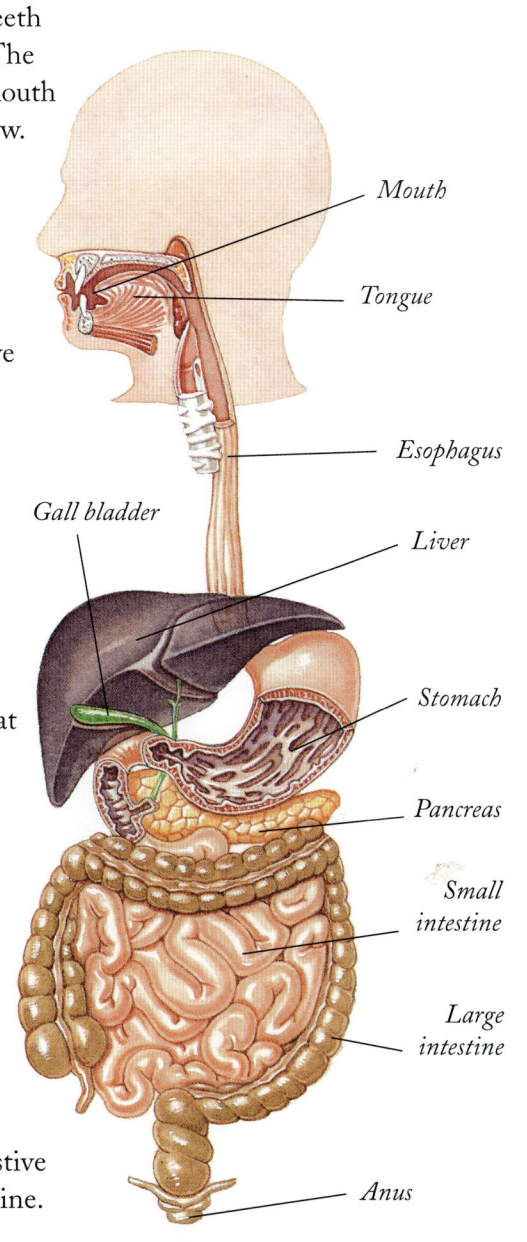

ENZYMES

Digestive juices made in your mouth, stomach, and small intestine contain enzymes (digestive chemicals). Enzymes break down the food you eat into nutrients that are small enough to pass through the walls of your small intestine and into your blood.

Eating Bread

There are three main types of food: **proteins**, **starches**, and **fats and oils**. The starch in bread is made of long chains of sugars. When you put bread in your mouth, enzymes in your saliva begin to break down the starch into smaller chains. If you chew some bread, saliva will flow into your mouth. After you have chewed for a while, the bread will taste sweet as your saliva breaks the starch into sugar. Enzymes in the small intestine (see page 10) eventually break down the starch chains into single sugars, which can be absorbed into the blood.

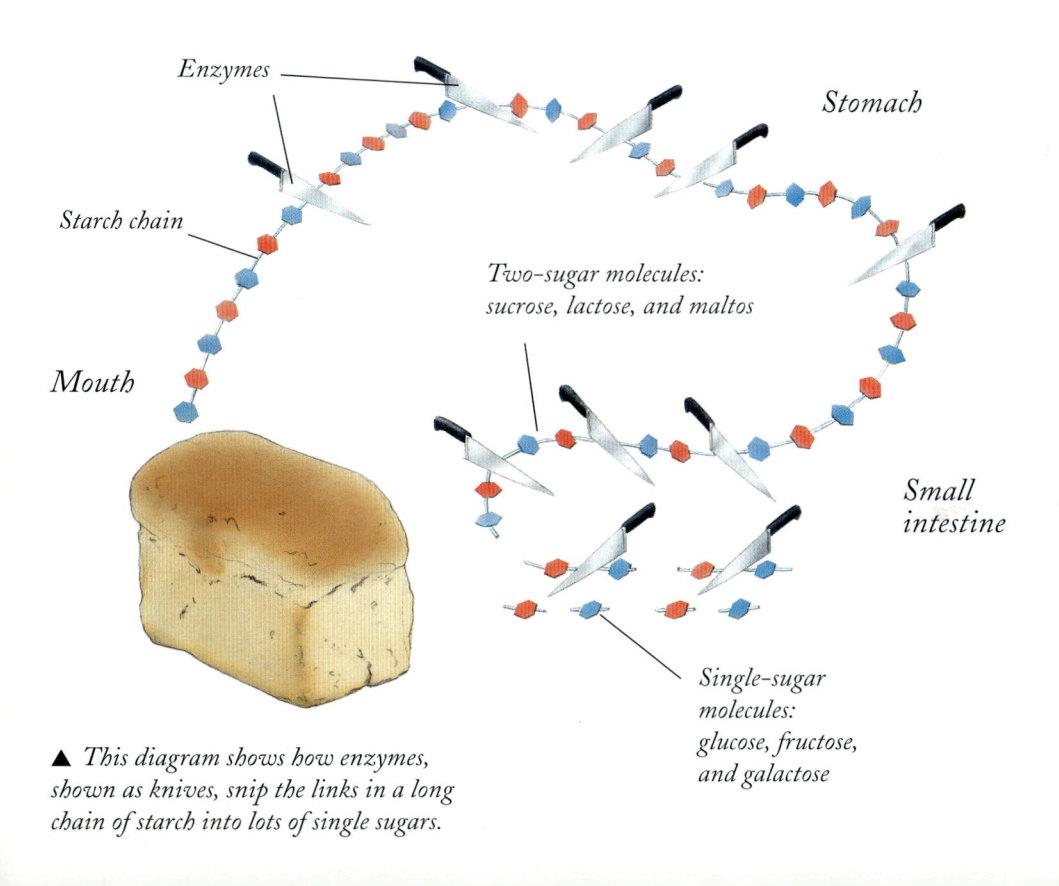

Enzymes

Stomach

Starch chain

Two-sugar molecules: sucrose, lactose, and maltos

Mouth

Small intestine

Single-sugar molecules: glucose, fructose, and galactose

▲ This diagram shows how enzymes, shown as knives, snip the links in a long chain of starch into lots of single sugars.

MOUTH

Food enters the digestive system through the mouth, where the action of chewing begins the digestive process.

Your mouth prepares food for its journey through the rest of the digestive system. Your teeth cut, tear, and grind food into small pieces. Your tongue helps mix the food with saliva, and then pushes the chewed pulp to the back of the throat ready for swallowing.

Teeth

Your teeth come in different shapes and sizes, and are extremely tough. The flat teeth at the front are called **incisors**. They cut food into pieces that can fit into your mouth. The **canines** are pointed to grip and tear food. Your **pre-molars** and **molars** are large and flat-topped. They crush and grind your food into a pulp.

▲ *A baby's first teeth, called milk teeth, begin to appear at 6 months. Most children lose their milk teeth at about the age of six, as their permanent teeth come through.*

Molars

Wisdom tooth

Tongue

Pre-molars

Canine

Incisors

▲ *This mouth displays a full set of 32 permanent teeth. The last to appear are the wisdom teeth.*

Food

The nutrients in food give your body energy, and enable it to grow, and keep warm and healthy. The most important nutrients are protein, starch, fat, minerals, vitamins, fiber, and water.

Balanced Diet

If you only ever ate your favorite food, it probably would not give you everything your body needs. To keep healthy, you need to eat a mixture of foods. This mixture should include large amounts of carbohydrate (starch and sugars) and protein, and smaller amounts of fat.

Vitamins

You need small amounts of vitamins to help your body grow and to keep fit. For instance, **Vitamin A** helps your eyesight. It is found in fruit and yellow vegetables. **Vitamin C** keeps your skin and gums healthy. It also helps you to heal. It is found in fresh fruit, particularly oranges.

Eggs, milk, fish, and meat are rich in protein, which helps your body grow and heal

Butter and oil are rich in fat, which gives you energy and helps you keep warm

Fresh fruit and vegetables provide fiber, which helps the digestive system work properly

Fresh fruit and vegetables also provide vitamins, and minerals

Rice, pasta, bread, and beans are rich in carbohydrates, which give you energy

▲ *This food pyramid shows what proportion of each type of food represents a balanced healthy diet.*

KIDNEYS AND BLADDER

As your body uses up nutrients, it produces waste products such as carbon dioxide, salt, and other harmful chemicals. Most of this waste is filtered out of your blood by your kidneys. Your kidneys and bladder are shown on your urinary system acetate.

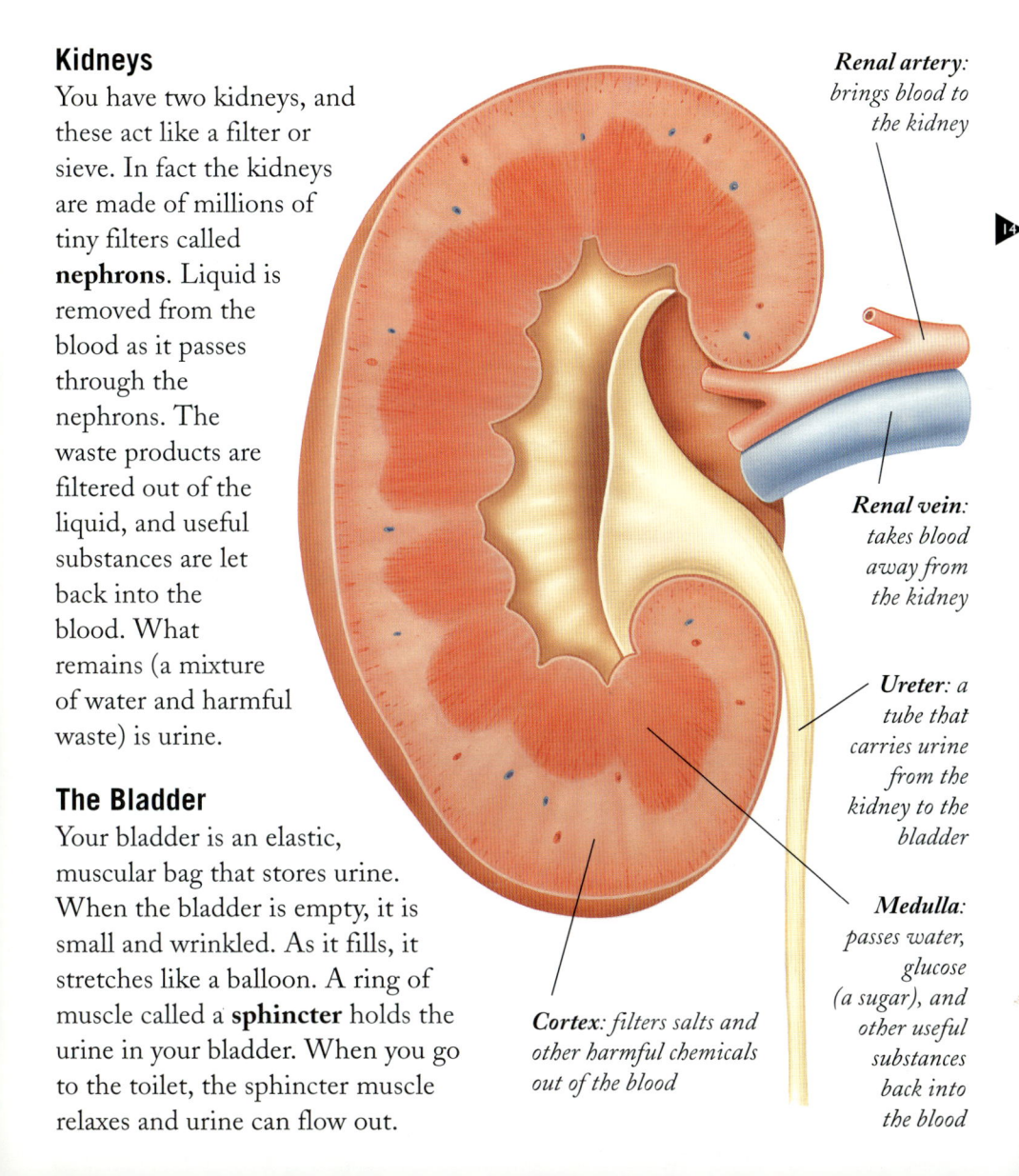

Kidneys

You have two kidneys, and these act like a filter or sieve. In fact the kidneys are made of millions of tiny filters called **nephrons**. Liquid is removed from the blood as it passes through the nephrons. The waste products are filtered out of the liquid, and useful substances are let back into the blood. What remains (a mixture of water and harmful waste) is urine.

The Bladder

Your bladder is an elastic, muscular bag that stores urine. When the bladder is empty, it is small and wrinkled. As it fills, it stretches like a balloon. A ring of muscle called a **sphincter** holds the urine in your bladder. When you go to the toilet, the sphincter muscle relaxes and urine can flow out.

Renal artery: brings blood to the kidney

Renal vein: takes blood away from the kidney

Ureter: a tube that carries urine from the kidney to the bladder

Medulla: passes water, glucose (a sugar), and other useful substances back into the blood

Cortex: filters salts and other harmful chemicals out of the blood

WATER

Sixty percent of your body weight is water. Every cell in your body contains water, and your body's transport systems rely on water. It is essential that your body controls its water balance.

Keeping the Balance

Your kidneys help to keep the right amount of water in your body. When you drink more liquid than your body can use, your kidneys make more urine, which your body releases when you go to the toilet (see page 14). If you have not been drinking enough or have lost water through sweating, your brain sends a message to your body that makes you feel thirsty and have a drink. A hormone called **aldosterone** (see page 16) instructs your kidneys not to filter so much water from your blood.

▼ *These two bottles show the average flow of water in and out of your body every day. Each bottle represents 1½ pints.*

Sweating

Sweating helps keep your body cool after physical exercise, in hot weather, or when you have a high temperature. It also means your body loses water.

▲ *Most marathon runners drink plenty of liquids during a race to replace the water lost through sweating.*

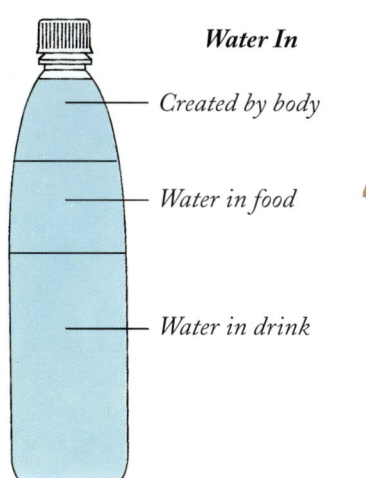

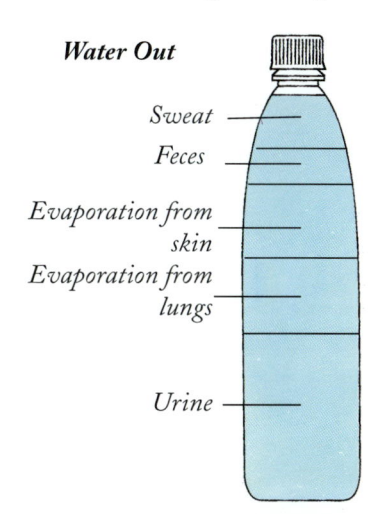

Water In
- Created by body
- Water in food
- Water in drink

Water Out
- Sweat
- Feces
- Evaporation from skin
- Evaporation from lungs
- Urine

HORMONES

Your brain sends messages to your body in two different ways. The nervous system sends high-speed electrical messages for immediate reaction (see page 7). The hormone system sends slower, chemical messages that work over a longer time.

Endocrine Glands

Hormones are released from **endocrine glands**. The pituitary gland at the base of your brain is the most important. Look at the two hormonal system acetates to see where the main endocrine glands are in a man's and in a woman's body.

◀ *Pituitary gland*: produces a hormone that makes your body grow. It also controls most of the other glands.

◀ *Thyroid gland*: produces a hormone that controls how fast your body uses up energy.

▲ *Testes*: a gland in males that produces testosterone. This causes physical changes in teenage boys. Their voices become deeper and more hair grows on their bodies.

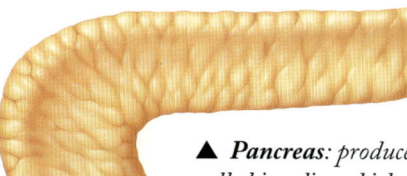

▲ *Pancreas*: produces a hormone called insulin which controls the sugar level in your blood. Too little insulin can cause diabetes.

▲ *Ovaries*: glands in females that produce estrogen. This causes teenage girls to grow breasts and enables them to have babies.

▶ *Adrenal glands*: produce a hormone called adrenalin, which makes you ready to run away or fight when you are scared. They also produce aldosterone, a hormone that makes you thirsty if your body needs water.

SEEING

You find out what is going on around you through your five senses. These are your sense of sight, hearing, smell, touch, and taste. Of these, your sense of sight is perhaps the most important.

Eyes
Your eyes are shaped like balls. They have a tough, white outer layer called **sclera**. For added protection, they are set inside two holes in your skull called eye sockets.

▼ *This cutaway diagram of an eye shows an upside-down image of a kite projected on the back of the retina.*

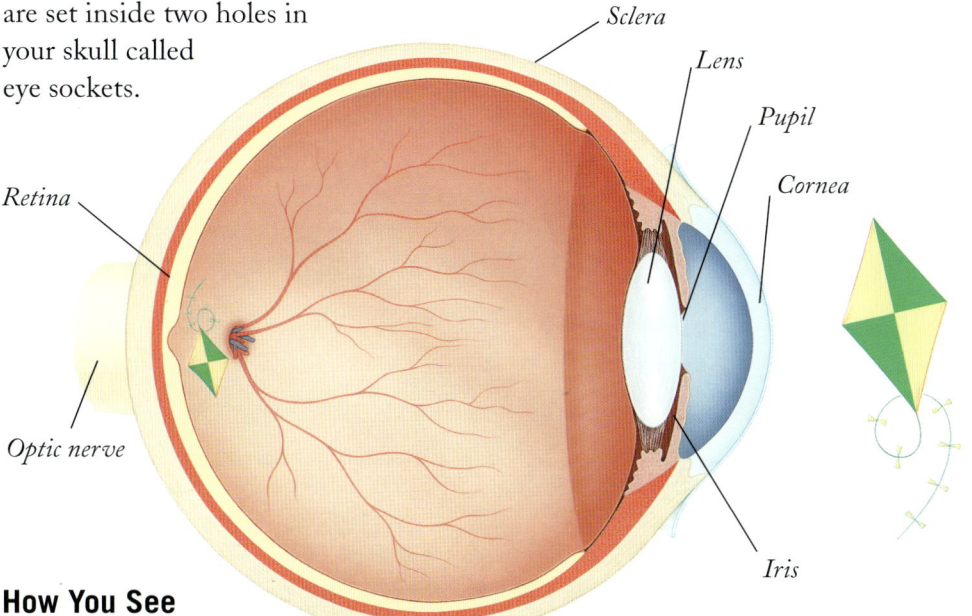

Sclera
Lens
Pupil
Cornea
Retina
Optic nerve
Iris

How You See
Light enters the front of your eye through the **cornea** and then through the hole in your **iris** called a **pupil**. The light is focused by the cornea and by the **lens** to form an upside-down image on the **retina** at the back of the eye. Nerve fibers in the retina send a message along the **optic nerve** to your brain. Your brain turns the image the right way up.

The Pupil
Your iris is the colored part of your eye, and it works like a shutter. In dim light, the iris retracts, or opens, to make the pupil bigger and let more light into your eye. In bright light, it expands, or closes, to stop the light damaging the sensitive retina cells.

HEARING

The parts of your ears that you can see are like ear trumpets. They collect sound waves from the air and direct them into the inner parts of your ears, which are inside your head.

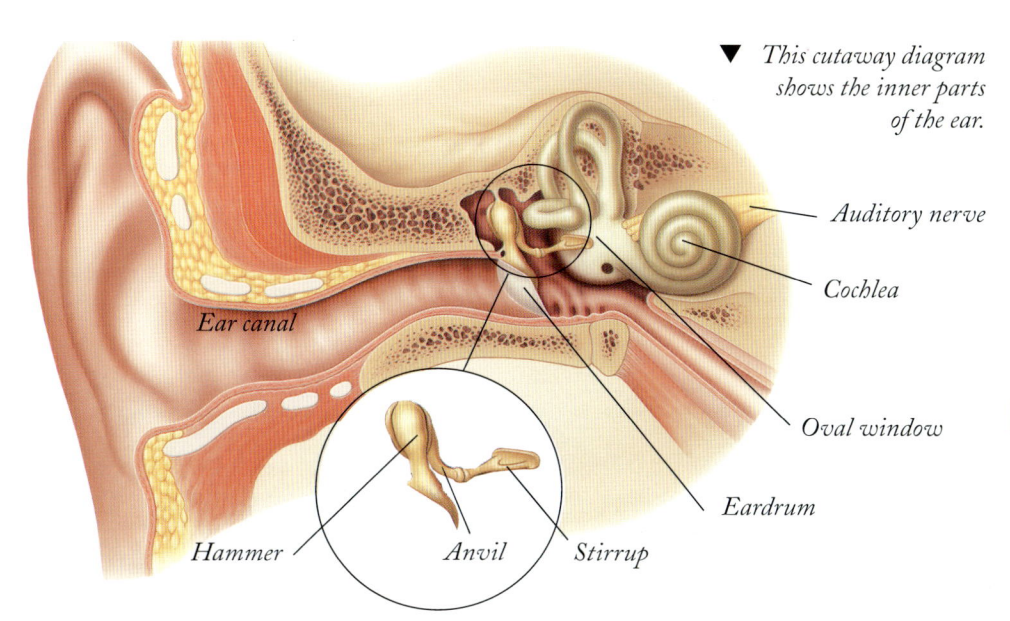

This cutaway diagram shows the inner parts of the ear.

Auditory nerve
Cochlea
Ear canal
Oval window
Eardrum
Hammer
Anvil
Stirrup

Sound Waves

A jet taking off, a guitar playing, a dog barking – all these things cause the air around them to travel towards you in waves, like the ripples made when a stone is thrown into a pond.

Hearing

Sound waves travel down the ear canal and hit the **eardrum**, making it vibrate. These rapid movements pass along tiny **ear bones**, called the hammer, anvil, and stirrup, to the **oval window**. This guards the entrance to the inner ear. As the stirrup bone pounds the oval window, it sets up vibrations in the liquid inside a coiled tube called the **cochlea**. The liquid vibrates and moves tiny hairs on the end of nerve cells in the **auditory nerve**. This nerve then sends the sounds as a message to the hearing center of the brain (see page 6).

Two Ears

Having two ears helps you tell where a sound comes from. Sound waves reach the ear nearest the thing making the noise just before they reach the ear farthest away. Your brain uses this tiny time difference to work out the direction of the sound.

Smell

Your nose and your brain work together to help you identify smells. Smells are caused by many of the tiny chemicals that float in the air. They go up your nose when you breathe in, or sniff.

Smelling

Between your nostrils and the back of your throat there is an air space or cavity with a patch of cells called **smell receptors**. Each cell has tiny hairs covered in a sticky substance called **mucus**. When you breathe in, chemicals in the air go up your nose and dissolve in the mucus. They are detected by the smell receptors, which send nerve messages to the brain.

Useful Sense of Smell

Your sense of smell can warn you of danger, or make you happy. Rotten food often has a terrible smell, which will put you off eating it. Leaking gas and smoke have strong smells, which can warn you of danger. Smelling food is an important part of tasting it. When you have a cold and your nose is blocked, you cannot smell your food and so it seems less tasty.

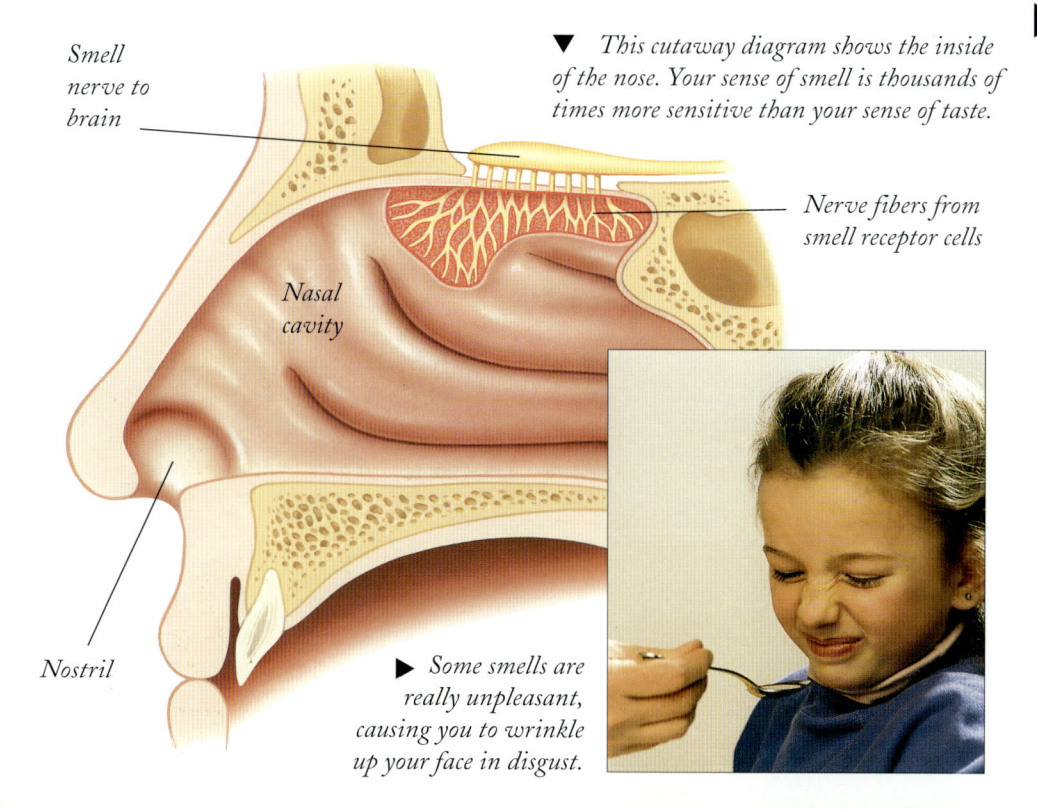

▼ *This cutaway diagram shows the inside of the nose. Your sense of smell is thousands of times more sensitive than your sense of taste.*

Smell nerve to brain

Nerve fibers from smell receptor cells

Nasal cavity

Nostril

▶ *Some smells are really unpleasant, causing you to wrinkle up your face in disgust.*

TASTE

The back of your throat, the roof of your mouth, but mainly the surface of your tongue are covered in taste buds, which detect tastes. Nerve cells in the taste buds send signals to your brain.

Different Tastes

Look at your tongue in a mirror. It is covered in lots of small bumps called **papillae**. Your taste buds, which are too small to see, are tucked in the gaps between these bumps. Each of your taste buds can only detect one of four basic kinds of taste: sweet, salty, sour, and bitter.

▼ *This picture shows where the different kinds of taste buds are on the tongue.*

Upper surface of tongue

Bitter Tastes

Taste buds at the back of your tongue detect bitter tastes. These taste buds can warn you of danger, since poison is often bitter. When you taste something bitter, you probably want to spit it out. This saves you from eating something that could make you ill.

Sour: *the sides of the tongue (shown yellow) detect sour tastes such as vinegar.*

Salty: *the front of the tongue (shown green) detects salty tastes.*

Sweet: *the tip of the tongue responds to sweetness.*

Bitter: *the back of the tongue (shown blue) picks up bitter tastes such as coffee grains.*

TOUCH

You feel the Sun's heat, the cold of ice, and the pain of a pinprick through touch sensors, or nerve endings, buried just under your skin.

Touch Sensors

There are millions of touch nerve endings under your skin, but they are not spread evenly all over your body. They are packed closely together in your fingertips, on your feet, and on your tongue and lips, which makes these areas most sensitive to touch. They are spread much further apart on your back and bottom.

▶ *In this picture, the most sensitive parts of the body have been enlarged.*

Under the Skin

The cutaway diagram of the skin below shows five kinds of touch nerve endings. Each of these detect different sensations. When nerve endings feel pressure, or heat or cold, they send messages to the touch center in your brain (see page 6). More than one kind of nerve ending is used for most things you feel, so you can tell the difference between similar sensations.

Bulb of Krause: feels extreme cold

Merkel's endings: feel light touch

Hair

Pacinian endings: feel heavy touch

Free nerve endings: feel most things

Meissner's ending: feels vibrations

A New Baby

A baby begins to grow when a sperm cell from a man joins together with an egg cell from a woman. The new cell that is made grows by constantly dividing into more cells, which grow into a tiny embryo.

How a Baby Starts

Each month an egg cell from one of a woman's ovaries (see page 16) travels along the **Fallopian tube** towards her **uterus**, or womb. If a sperm cell from a man's testes joins with the egg cell, the egg becomes fertilized and sticks itself to the soft wall of the uterus. Here it develops into a baby. It takes nine months for a baby to develop before it is ready to be born. This process is called pregnancy.

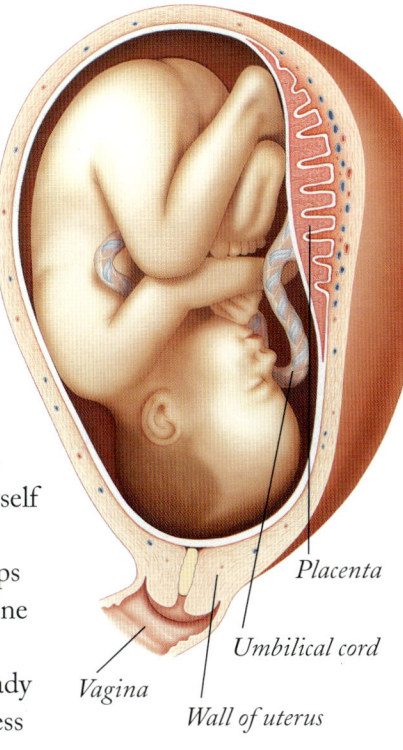

◀ *By nine months, most babies are positioned upside down in the uterus, ready to be born head first.*

Placenta
Umbilical cord
Vagina
Wall of uterus

In the Uterus

During pregnancy, the baby floats in a protective liquid called **amniotic fluid**. Food and oxygen pass from the mother to her baby along a tube called the **umbilical cord**. This links a mass of blood vessels called the **placenta** to the baby's belly. The placenta absorbs food and oxygen from the mother's blood.

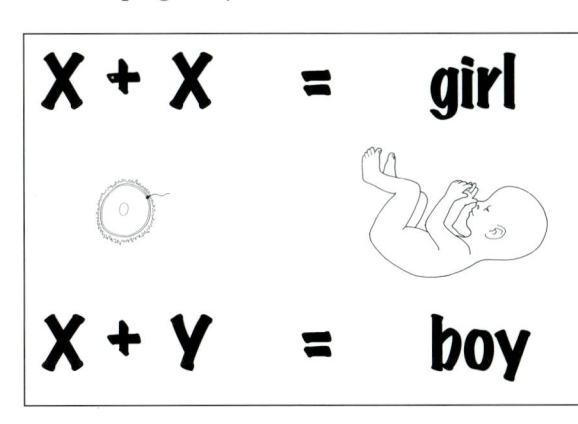

X + X = girl

X + Y = boy

Boy or Girl?

The sex of a baby is decided by the chromosomes (see page 23) carried by the egg cell and the sperm cell. All egg cells carry an "X" chromosome. Sperm cells carry either an "X" or a "Y" chromosome. If an "X" sperm fertilizes an egg, the baby will be a girl. If a "Y" sperm fertilizes an egg, the baby will be a boy.

Looking Alike

There are certain things about you, and about everyone else, that make each person quite different. This is because your cells contain a unique combination of chemical codes called **genes**.

The nucleus of our cells (see page 2) contains **chromosomes**. These are made of chains of chemicals called DNA. Each chain is made of individual instructions called genes. The way these instructions combine decides such things as the color of your eyes and hair.

▲ *All the people in this photograph belong to the same family. Can you spot the similarities between them?*

Family Likenesses

Children inherit some of their genes from their father and some from their mother. So though each child has its own unique set of genes, children tend to look like one or both of their parents.

Identical Twins

Identical twins, like those on the left, are born when a fertilized egg cell splits in two, and separate babies grow from each part. They look identical because each has inherited the same set of genes from its parents. Non-identical twins are born when two different eggs are fertilized by two sperm. These twins are no more alike than brothers and sisters born at different times.

GROWTH AND DEVELOPMENT

Most newborn babies are about 20 inches long. As they become older (those below are about six months old), they get taller and heavier, and steadily increase their physical and learning skills.

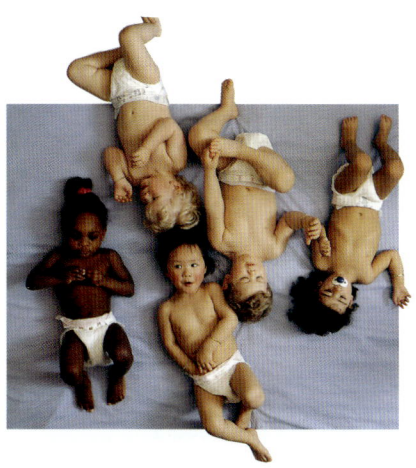

Changing Shape

When you were a baby, your head was very large compared to your body. It was about a quarter of your whole length. This is because the brain grows to nearly its full size by the time a child is three years old. When you are an adult, your head will be only an eighth of your whole length.

Growing Up

When boys are about 14 years old, and girls are about 12, they start to develop from children into adults. This period of change is called **puberty**, and it lasts for around four years. During puberty, boys develop deeper voices, grow taller and stronger, and begin to grow hair on their bodies. Girls develop breasts, wider hips, more rounded bodies, and start to release an egg from their ovaries each month (see page 22). If the egg is not fertilized, it leaves the girl's body during **menstruation**. This is often called having a period.

Growing Old

As people grow older, their bodies shrink slightly. Their hair may turn gray, and their skin may wrinkle and sag. Muscles become weaker, and bones more brittle and easily broken. Old people may have to walk with the aid of a stick.

◄ *These teenagers have reached the end of puberty.*

MUSCLES

Muscles enable all the movements your body makes. Your **skeletal muscles** are fixed to your bones by straps called **tendons**. These muscles are called **voluntary muscles** because you control them.

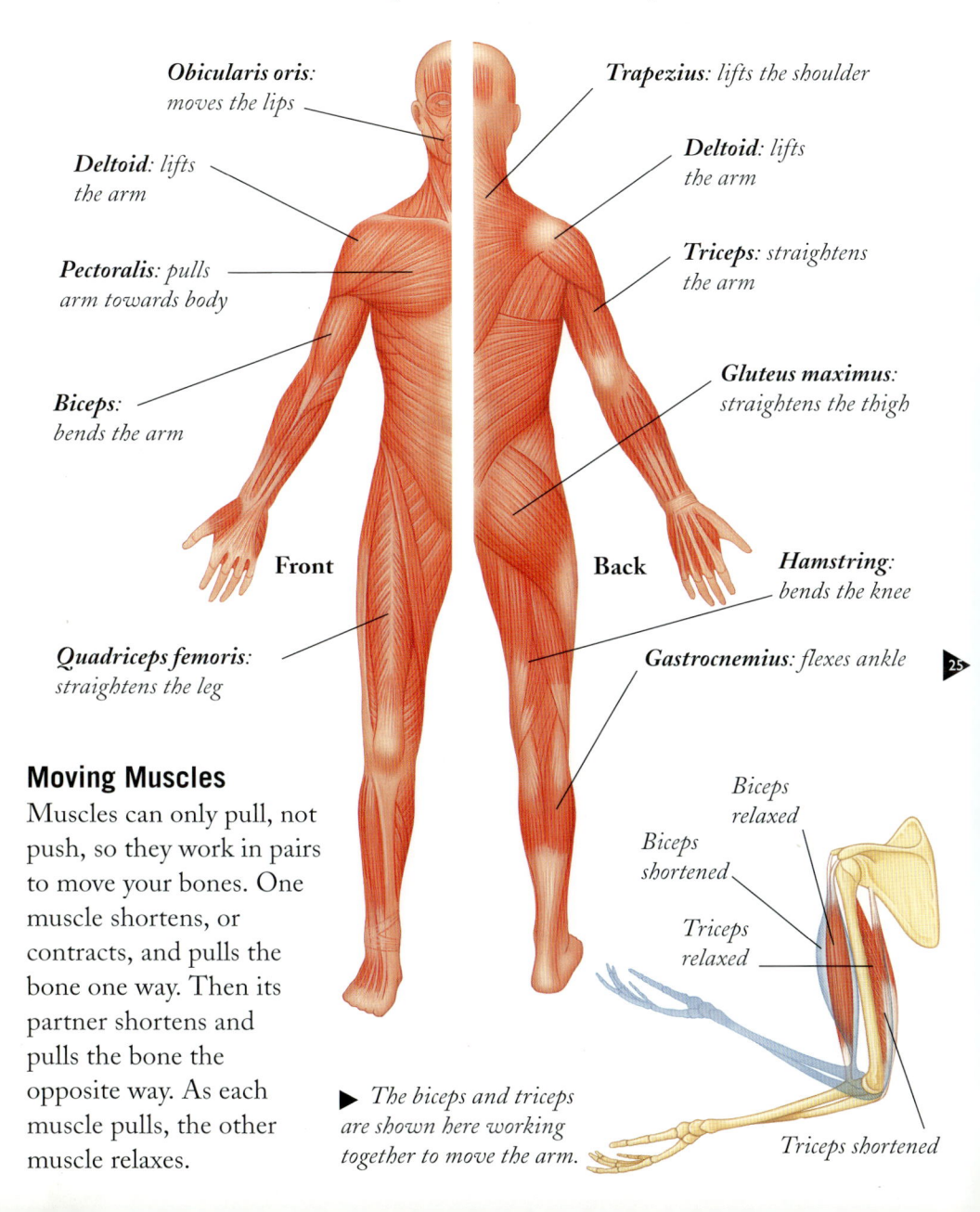

Obicularis oris: moves the lips

Deltoid: lifts the arm

Pectoralis: pulls arm towards body

Biceps: bends the arm

Quadriceps femoris: straightens the leg

Trapezius: lifts the shoulder

Deltoid: lifts the arm

Triceps: straightens the arm

Gluteus maximus: straightens the thigh

Hamstring: bends the knee

Gastrocnemius: flexes ankle

Front

Back

Moving Muscles

Muscles can only pull, not push, so they work in pairs to move your bones. One muscle shortens, or contracts, and pulls the bone one way. Then its partner shortens and pulls the bone the opposite way. As each muscle pulls, the other muscle relaxes.

▶ *The biceps and triceps are shown here working together to move the arm.*

Biceps relaxed
Biceps shortened
Triceps relaxed
Triceps shortened

INVOLUNTARY MUSCLES

Some muscles in your body work all day and all night, without you thinking about it. They are called **involuntary muscles**, and are not attached to bones, but are found in the internal organs.

Most involuntary muscles are made of **smooth muscle**. The walls of your esophagus (see page 10) are involuntary muscles. As soon as you swallow a mouthful of food, the smooth muscle of the esophagus shortens and relaxes in waves as it pushes the food to your stomach. This rhythmic movement is called **peristalsis**. Smooth muscle in your stomach and intestines continues to work while your food is digested. Smooth muscle is also responsible for squeezing urine from the bladder (see page 14), and pushing a baby from the uterus during birth (see page 22).

▼ *The smooth muscle of the esophagus can push food from your throat to your stomach in about 10 seconds.*

Your Heart

When you have been climbing a hill or carrying a heavy bag, the muscles in your legs and arms ache and feel tired. Your heart is made of a special type of involuntary muscle called **cardiac muscle**. This shortens and relaxes to make your heart beat between 60 and 100 times a minute every day of your life (see page 3).

◄ *Doctors use an instrument called a stethoscope to listen to a patient's heartbeat.*

SKELETON

Your skeleton is a framework for your body. It determines your body's shape, supports your muscles, and protects delicate organs.

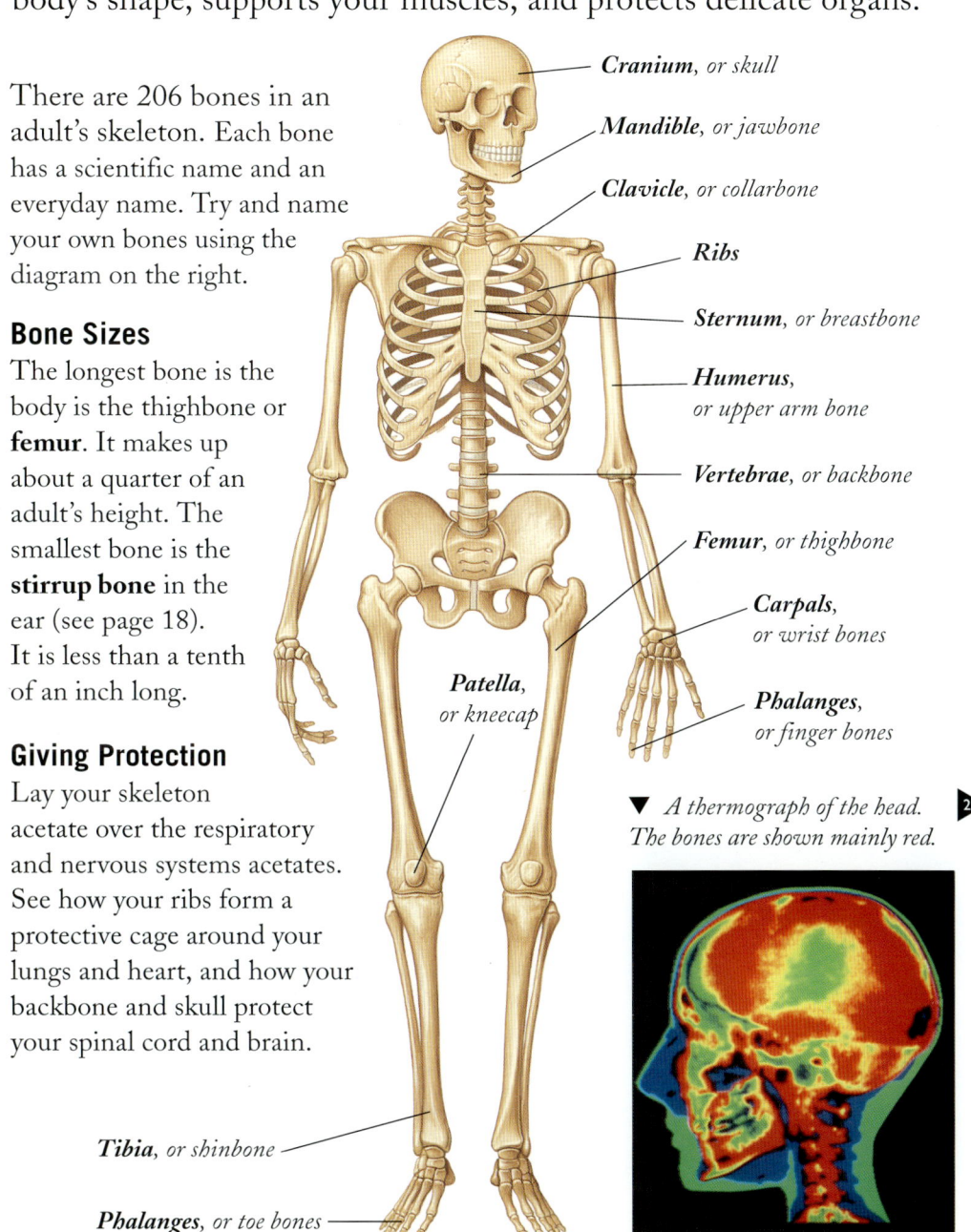

There are 206 bones in an adult's skeleton. Each bone has a scientific name and an everyday name. Try and name your own bones using the diagram on the right.

Bone Sizes

The longest bone is the body is the thighbone or **femur**. It makes up about a quarter of an adult's height. The smallest bone is the **stirrup bone** in the ear (see page 18). It is less than a tenth of an inch long.

Giving Protection

Lay your skeleton acetate over the respiratory and nervous systems acetates. See how your ribs form a protective cage around your lungs and heart, and how your backbone and skull protect your spinal cord and brain.

Cranium, or skull
Mandible, or jawbone
Clavicle, or collarbone
Ribs
Sternum, or breastbone
Humerus, or upper arm bone
Vertebrae, or backbone
Femur, or thighbone
Carpals, or wrist bones
Phalanges, or finger bones
Patella, or kneecap
Tibia, or shinbone
Phalanges, or toe bones

▼ *A thermograph of the head. The bones are shown mainly red.*

JOINTS

Although each of your bones is rigid, your skeleton is not. You can bend, run, clench your fist, and make all kinds of complicated movements because you have **joints** where your bones meet.

Bones are held together by strong, elastic straps called **ligaments**, which stretch as you move. The surfaces of the joints are covered in a smooth, shiny substance, called **cartilage**, to stop them grinding as they move. **Synovial fluid**, a slippery liquid, oils the joints to keep them working freely.

Types of Joints

Your body has many types of joint, each of which can carry out its own range of movements. The diagrams below show the main types of joint found in your body.

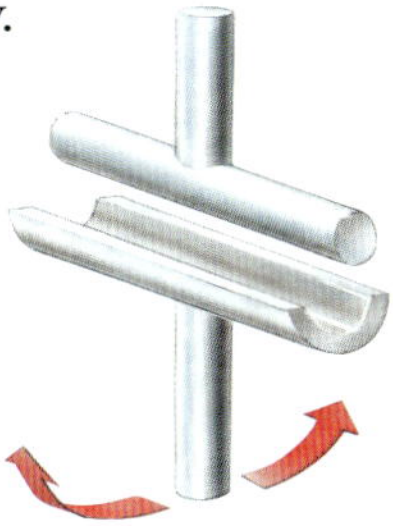

▶ *Pivot joint: found at the top of the spine. It lets you turn your head from side to side.*

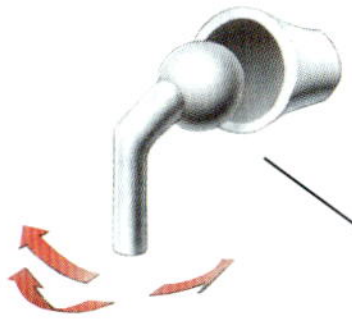

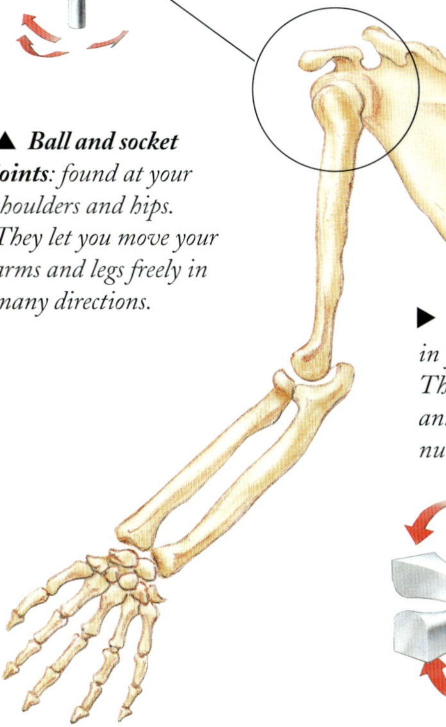

▲ *Ball and socket joints: found at your shoulders and hips. They let you move your arms and legs freely in many directions.*

◀ *Hinge joints: found at your elbows, knees, and fingers. They can only move back and forth in one direction.*

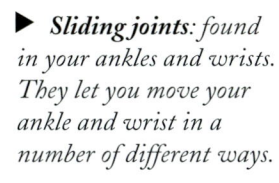

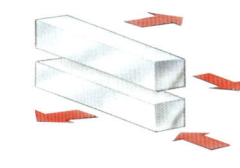

▶ *Sliding joints: found in your ankles and wrists. They let you move your ankle and wrist in a number of different ways.*

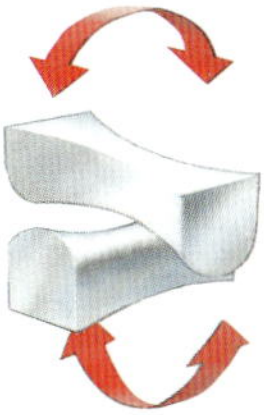

◀ *Saddle joints: found at the base of your thumbs. They let you move your thumbs up and down and side to side.*

BONES

Your bones are alive. They grow while you are young, and when they break they mend themselves. The core of bones is made of soft, fatty tissue, called **marrow**, which makes new blood cells.

Bone cells, like other living cells, need food and oxygen from blood. The blood vessels that supply the bone cells pass through tiny holes in the bone's tough skin, called the **periosteum**.

▼ *This cutaway diagram of a bone shows that bones are not solid.*

Strong Bones

Bone is strong and light. If you tested the strength of a bone and a steel bar of the same weight, the bone would be five times stronger! The tough outer part of the bone is made of strong fibers, and minerals such as calcium.

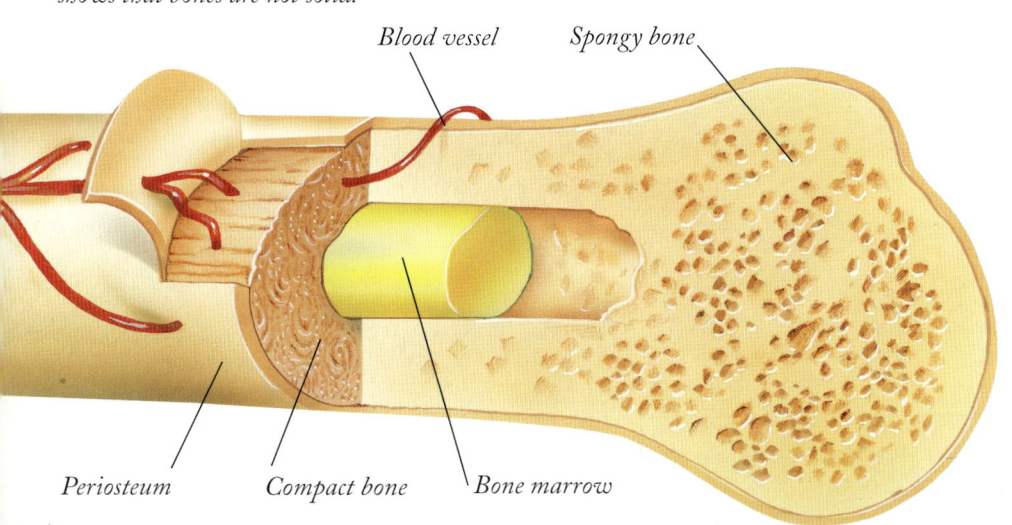

Blood vessel — *Spongy bone*

Periosteum — *Compact bone* — *Bone marrow*

Broken Bones

When you break a bone, an X-ray can be taken to show the break. The bone is then put back in line and kept in place with a plaster cast. In time, bone cells move into the break and repair the fracture. It takes about three months before the new cells harden, and the plaster cast can be removed.

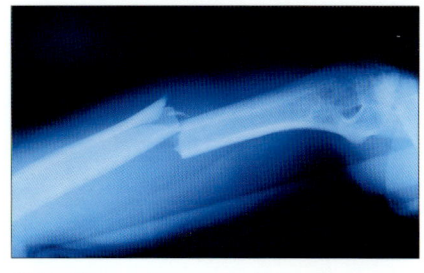

This X-ray shows a broken upper arm.

SKIN

Your skin is much more than just a covering for your body. It forms a barrier against germs. It stops water entering your body. But lets water out, as sweat, to help keep your temperature even.

Look at the cutaway diagram of the skin on the right. The outer layer of the skin is called the **epidermis**. Its surface is made up of dead skin cells. Below the surface, new cells grow to take their place. The inner layer of skin is called the **dermis**. This contains **sebaceous glands**, which produce an oil to keep your skin supple, and **sweat glands**, which pour sweat onto the surface of your skin. The dermis also contains hair follicles, which produce hairs.

Skin Color

The epidermis makes a pigment, called **melanin**, that helps to protect your skin from the rays of the sun. The more melanin you have, the darker your skin will be.

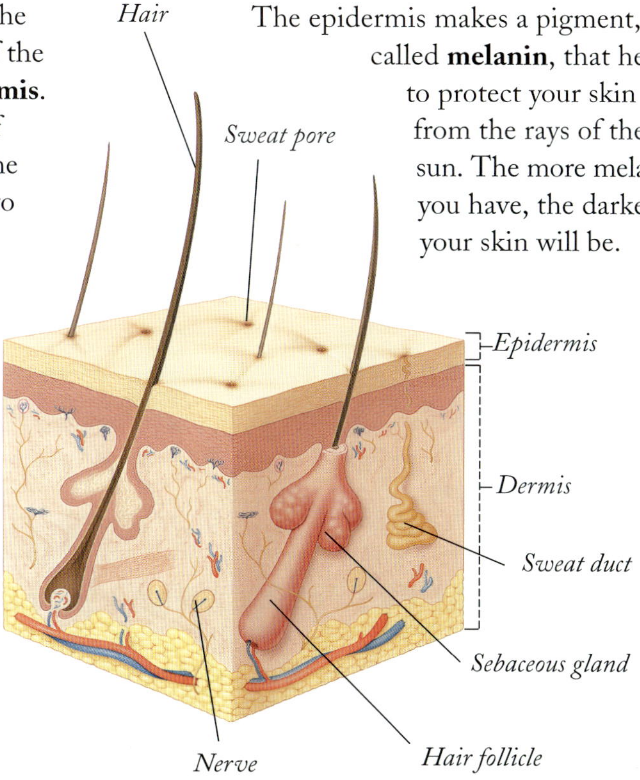

Hair
Sweat pore
Epidermis
Dermis
Sweat duct
Sebaceous gland
Hair follicle
Nerve

▼ *Although every fingerprint is unique, each one is made up of one of these four basic patterns.*

The arch *The whorl* *The loop* *The composite*

HAIR AND NAILS

The part of your hair and nails that you can see is made from dead cells reinforced by a tough protein called **keratin**. Hair and nails have no feeling in them, so it does not hurt when you cut them.

Your hair and nails may be dead, but they still grow. Hair grows from living follicles under the skin (see page 30). Nails grow from living cells in the nail root. Hair grows about 4 inches a year. Some hairs fall out everyday, but new ones usually grow back. Fingernails grow about 0.02 inches a week, which is three times faster than toenails. Both grow quicker in summer than in winter.

Hair at Work
The hair on your head protects your scalp from the sun. Your eyebrows stop sweat from dripping into your eyes. Eyelashes help keep dust out of your eyes. Hair in your nostrils helps to protect your nasal cavity from dirt.

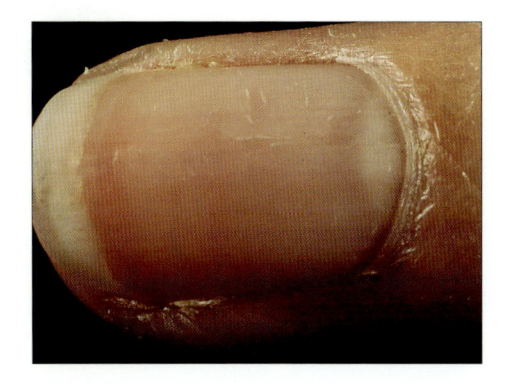

▼ *A hair follicle and a hair greatly magnified.*

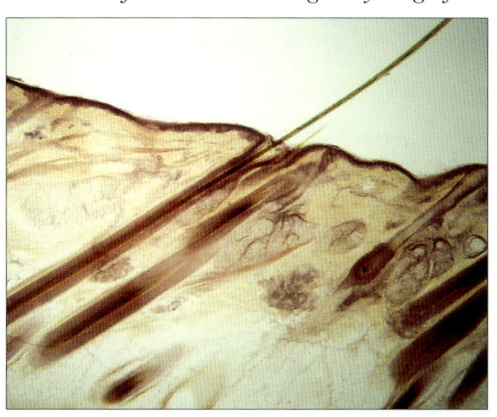

Studying Hair
You have millions of hairs growing on your body, and around 100,000 on the top of your head. But there are some parts of your body where no hair grows at all. Use the magnifier in the tray to study your skin. Where, apart from your head, do most hairs grow? Where do you have no hairs?

Straight or Curly
The shape of hair depends on the kind of follicle it grows from. Straight hair grows from a round follicle and has a circular shaft. Curly hair grows from a flat follicle and has a ribbon-like shaft. Wavy hair grows from an oval follicle and has an oval shaft. Use the magnifier to look at each type of hair.

▲ *Your fingernails protect the top surface of your fingertips, and help provide extra grip.*

Comparing Cells

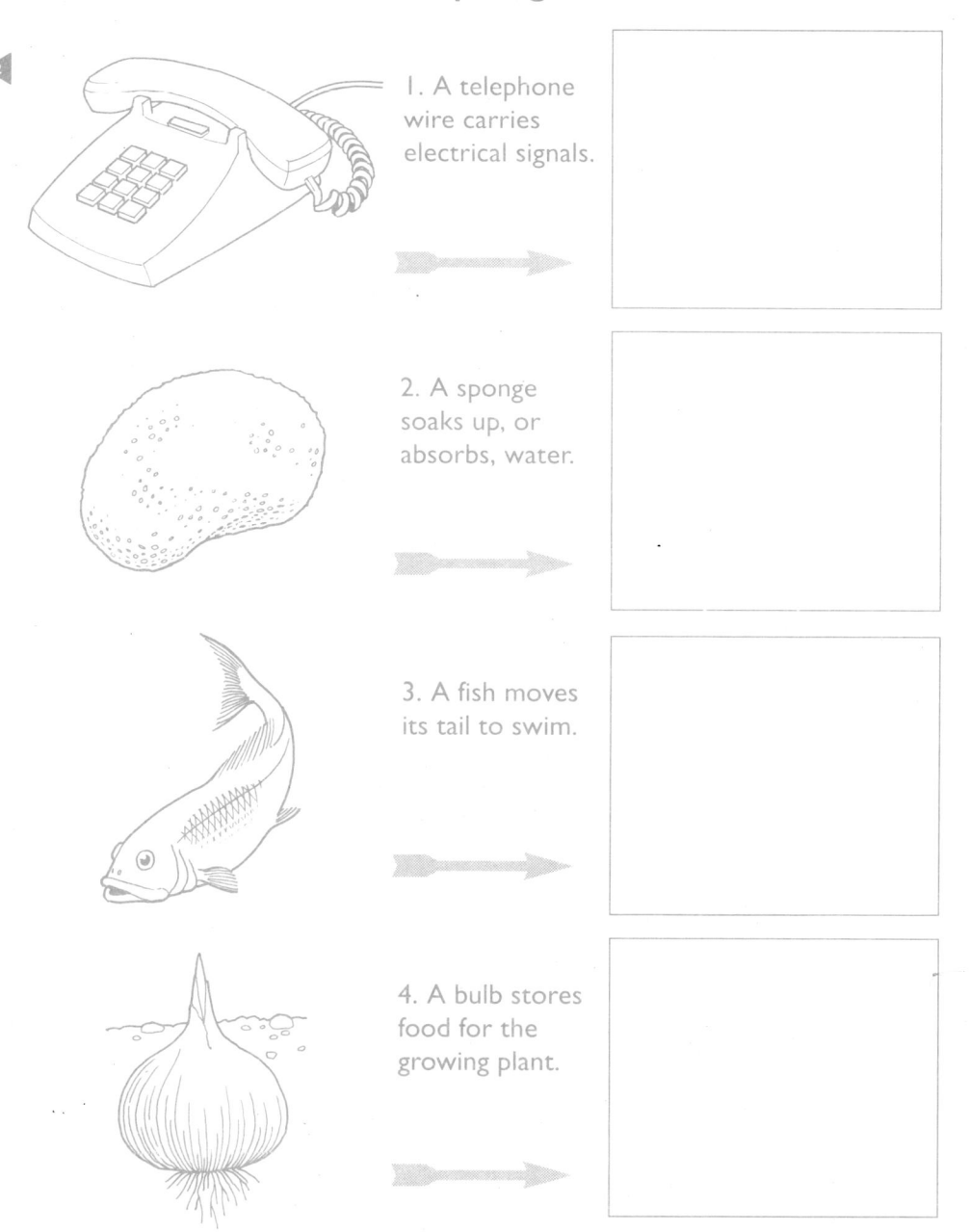

1. A telephone wire carries electrical signals.

2. A sponge soaks up, or absorbs, water.

3. A fish moves its tail to swim.

4. A bulb stores food for the growing plant.

The objects shown above work in a similar way to four of the body cells pictured on the opposite page. Match a cell to the appropriate object by drawing a cell in the box opposite the object that works most like it.

Time Your Heartbeat

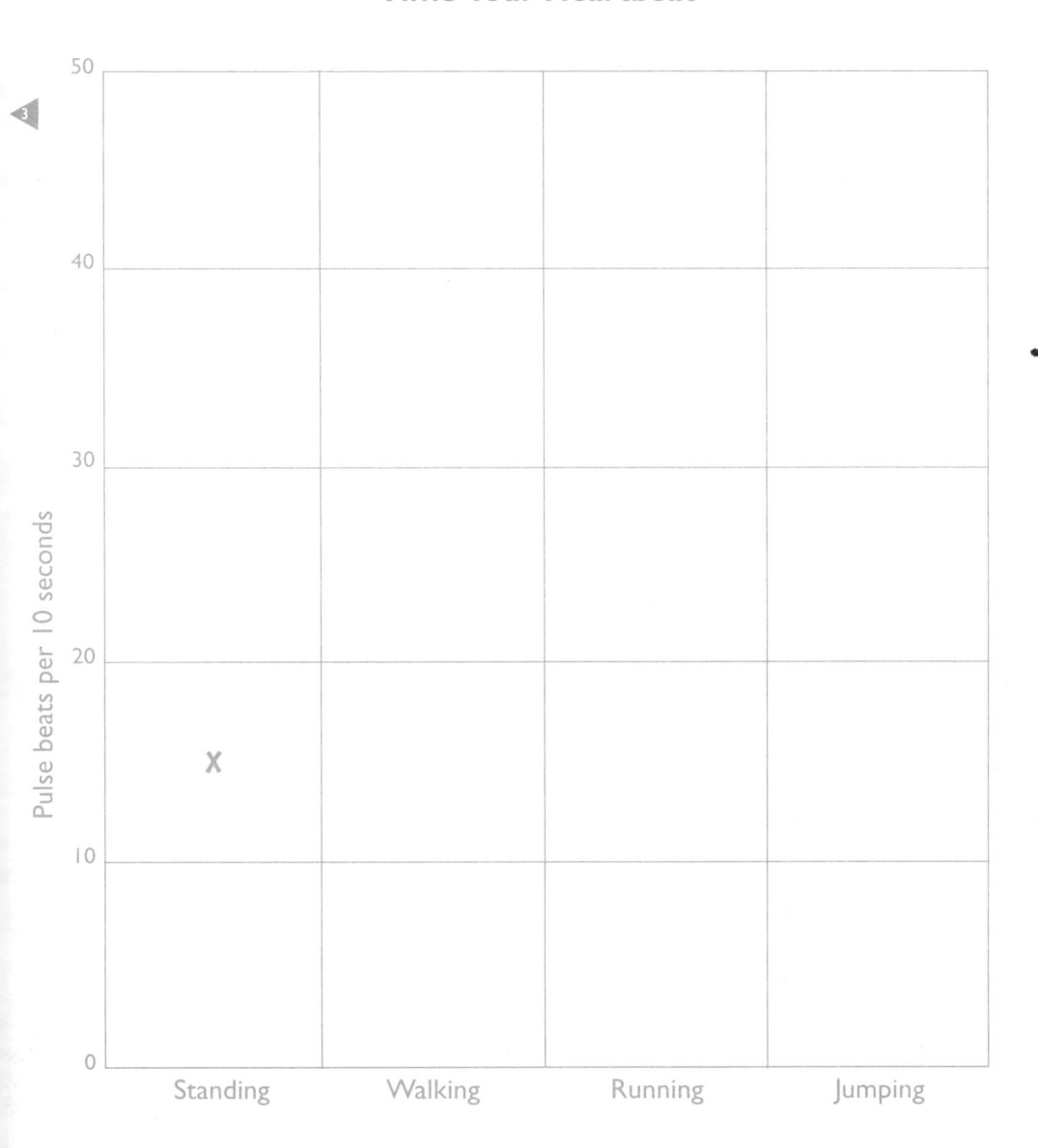

Pulse beats per 10 seconds (y-axis: 0 to 50)

x-axis categories: Standing, Walking, Running, Jumping

An X is plotted at Standing, 15 pulse beats per 10 seconds.

1. Stand still for 10 seconds.
2. Walk briskly for one minute.
3. Run for one minute.
4. Jump up and down for one minute.

Carry out each of these four activities. After each one, feel your pulse and count the number of beats in 10 seconds. Plot the results as a line graph on the grid above. We have plotted the pulse of an average child at rest, as an example.

Body Organs Sticker Activity

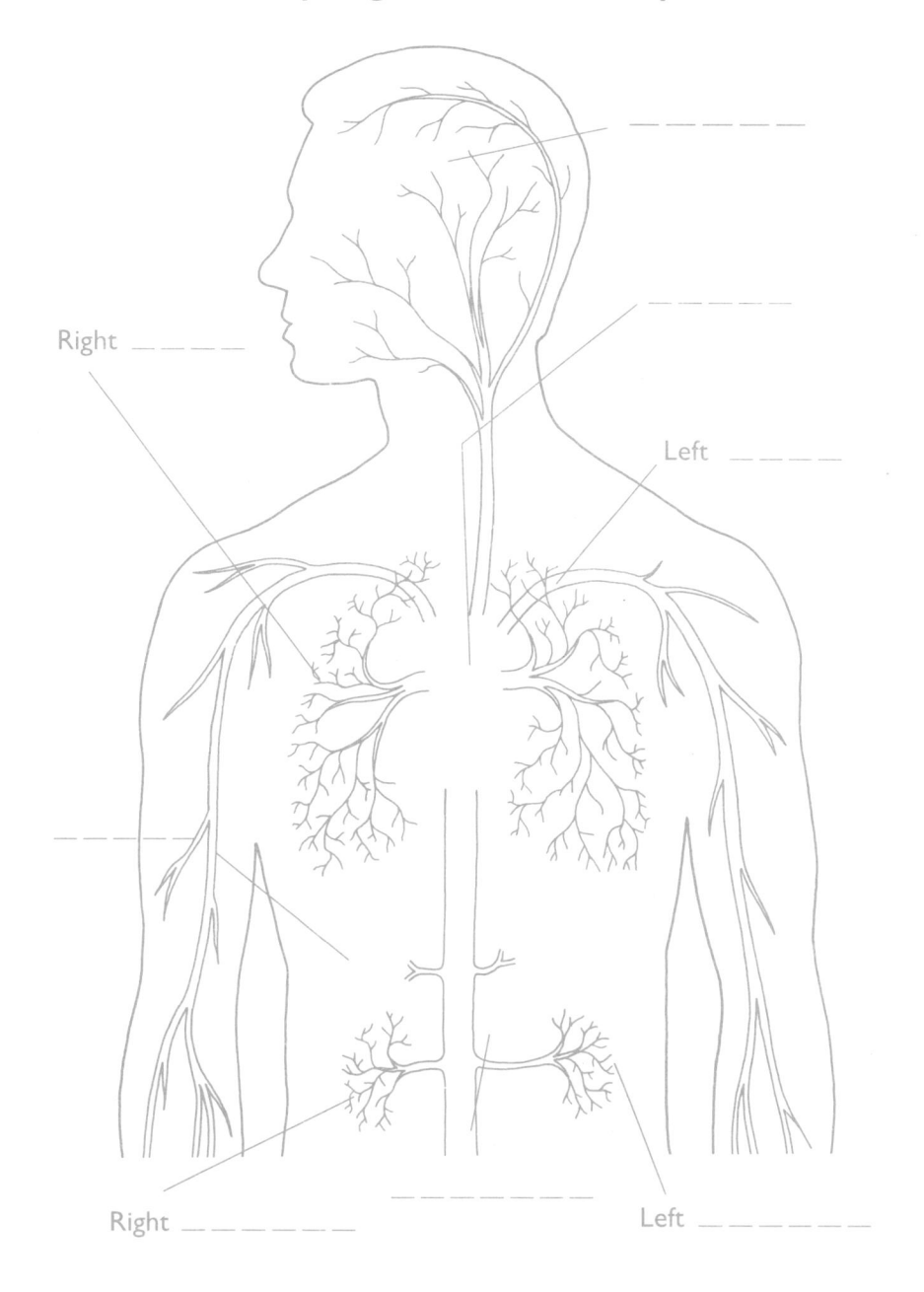

Right _____

Left _____

Right _____   Left _____

Place each organ sticker in its correct position on the body outline shown above. Use the blood vessels on the outline as a guide, and look at your acetate sheets to help you. Then label each organ. Go to pages 6, 8, 10, and 14 for more help.

Blood Cell Sticker Activity

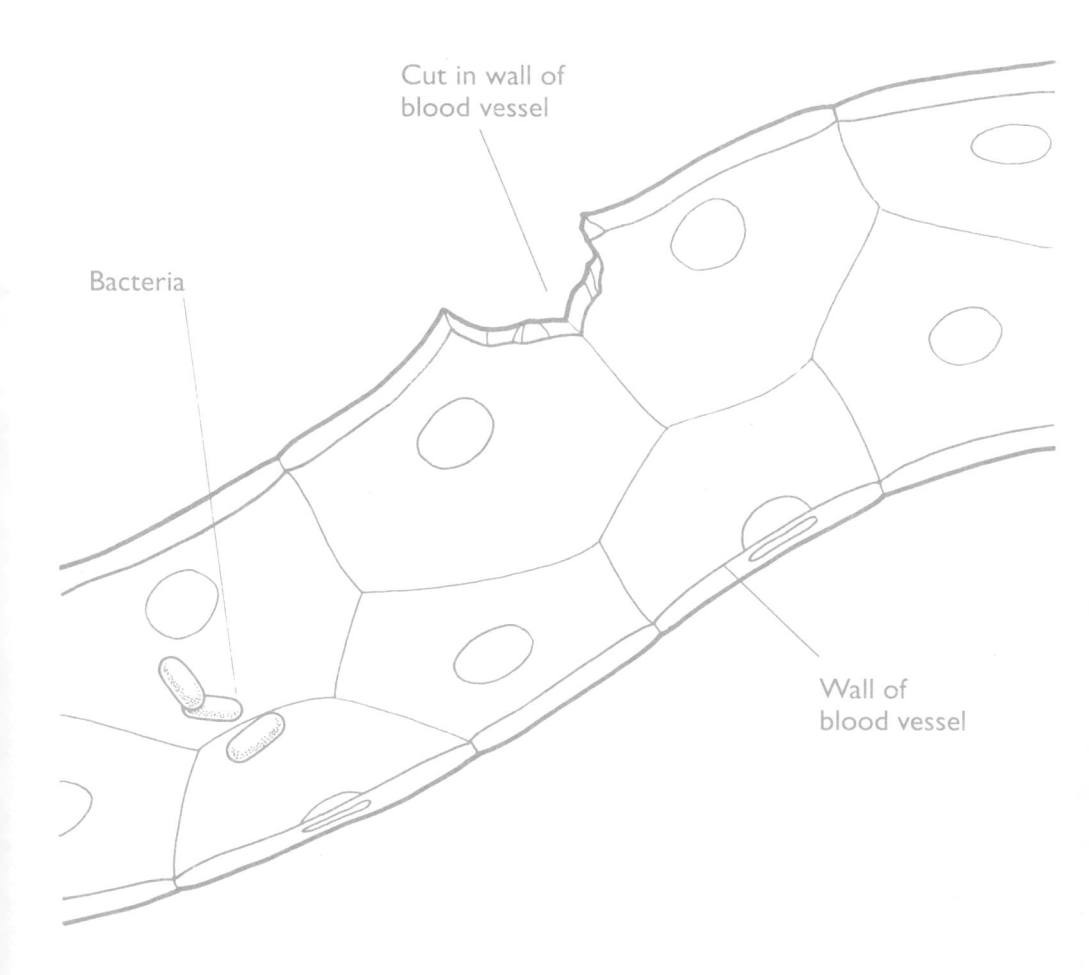

Cut in wall of blood vessel

Bacteria

Wall of blood vessel

Find your blood cell stickers. Place the blood-vessel cell sticker on the matching cell outline above. Then place the other cell stickers in an appropriate position within the blood vessel. The information on the opposite page will help you.

Test Your Memory

A

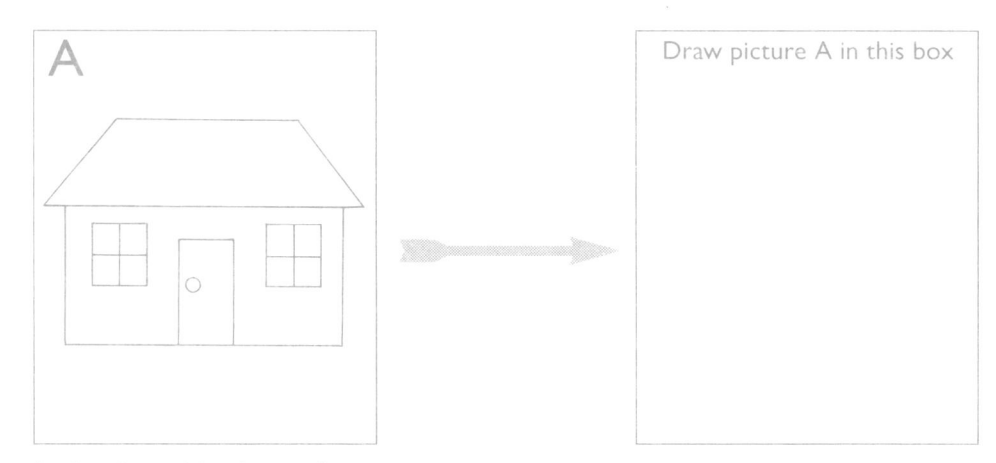

Draw picture A in this box

1. Look at this picture for 5 seconds. Cover it up and draw the picture in the box opposite, from memory.

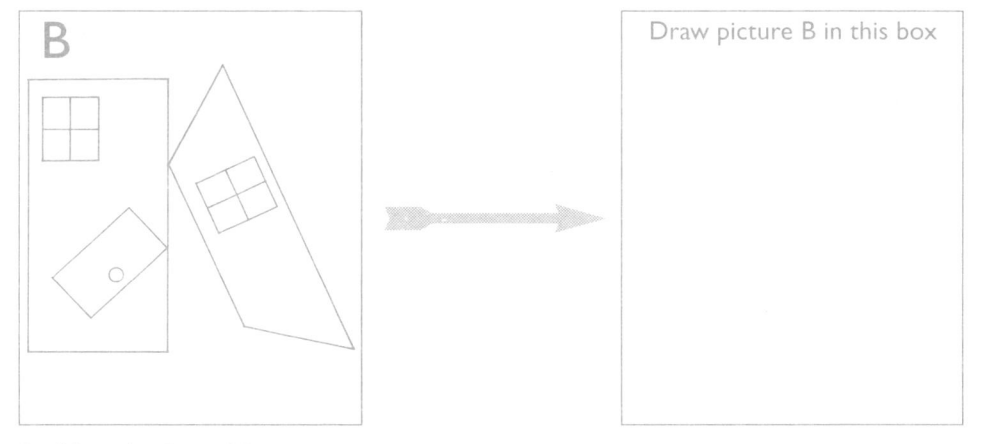

B

Draw picture B in this box

2. Now look at this pattern for 5 seconds. Then cover it up and draw the pattern from memory as well.

The pictures above are made from exactly the same shapes. Your brain finds it easier to remember things that have a pattern it can recognize. Do the two activities above to test your memory. Which picture did you remember best?

Identifying Reflex Actions

Action	Reflex action	Non-reflex action
1. Dropping a very hot plate	✔	
2. Catching a falling plate		
3. Sneezing		
4. Pulling thumb away from a pin prick		
5. Blinking to protect eyes from a fly		
6. Scratching an itch		
7. Hitting a tennis ball		
8. Swatting away a fly from your face		

The chart above lists eight different actions. Describe which are reflex actions and which are non-reflex actions (actions you choose to make) by putting a check in the appropriate box. We have done the first one for you.

Oxygen Experiment

WARNING — make sure an adult is present. Do not use matches yourself.

1. Find two clean, empty jars of the same size, and mark one "A" and the other "B."

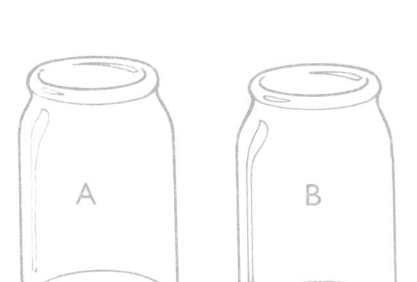

2. Hold jar "A" over your mouth for a minute so that it fills up with the air you breathe out. Leave jar "B" so that it only contains room air.

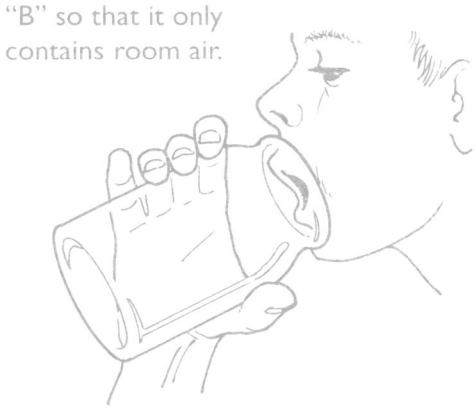

3. Ask an adult to light two small candles. Notice how they both burn evenly because oxygen is present in the air.

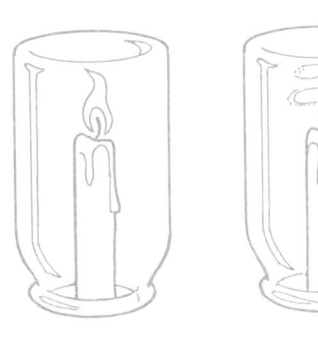

4. Now ask the adult to place a jar over each candle at the same time and see what happens.

The candle that went out first was in which jar? _____

Name the main gas in jar "A" after you breathed into it. _____

Try this simple experiment, *with the help of an adult*, and then answer the two questions above. Put a mark on one jar, so you don't confuse it with the other.

Time Your Breathing

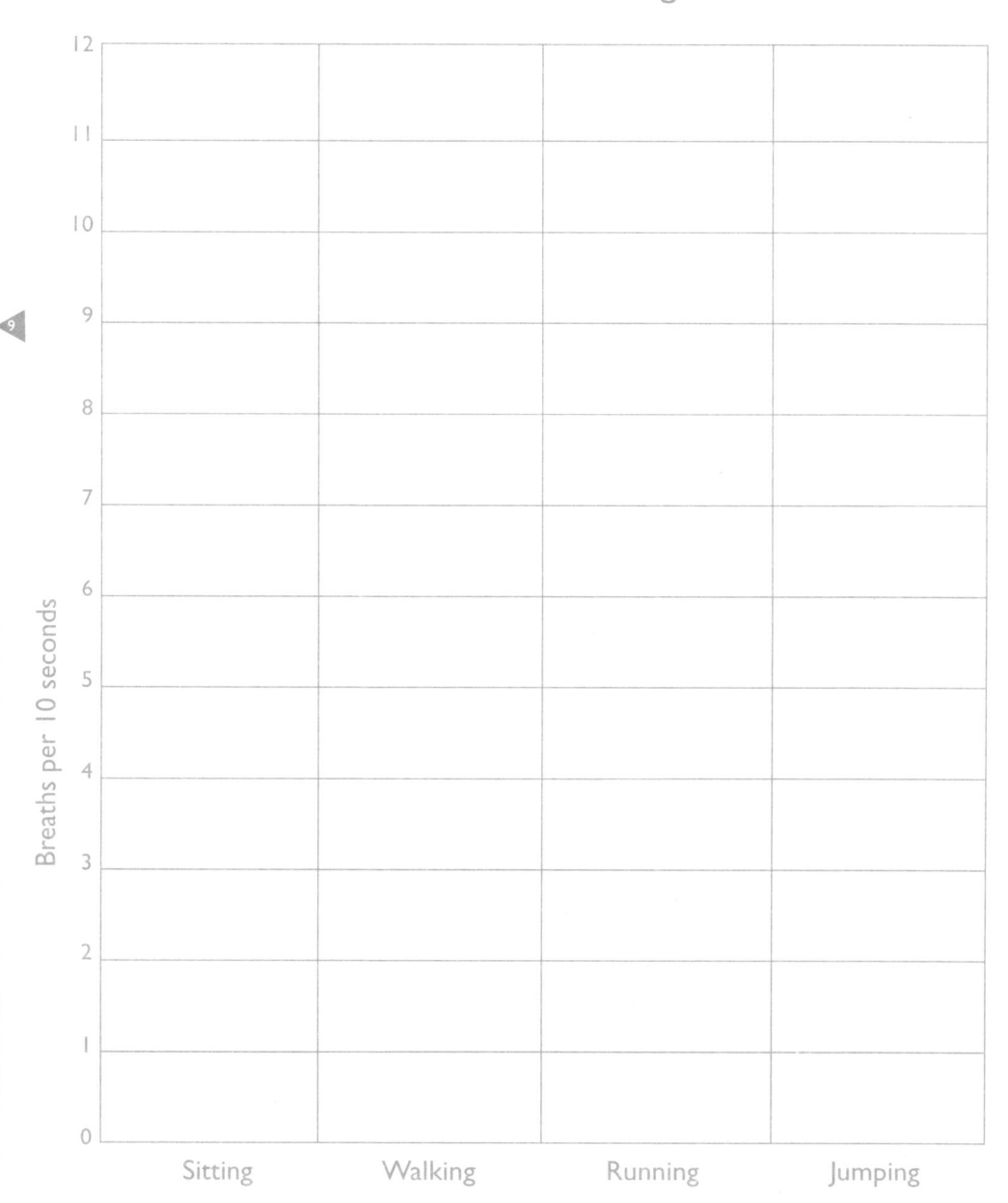

Breaths per 10 seconds (y-axis: 0 to 12)

x-axis categories: Sitting, Walking, Running, Jumping

1. Stand still for 10 seconds.
2. Walk briskly for one minute.
3. Run for one minute.
4. Jump up and down for one minute.

Carry out each of these four activities. After each one, count how many breaths you take in 10 seconds. Plot the results as a line graph on the grid above. Compare the graph you have made with the one you did on page 3.

Digestive System Sticker Activity

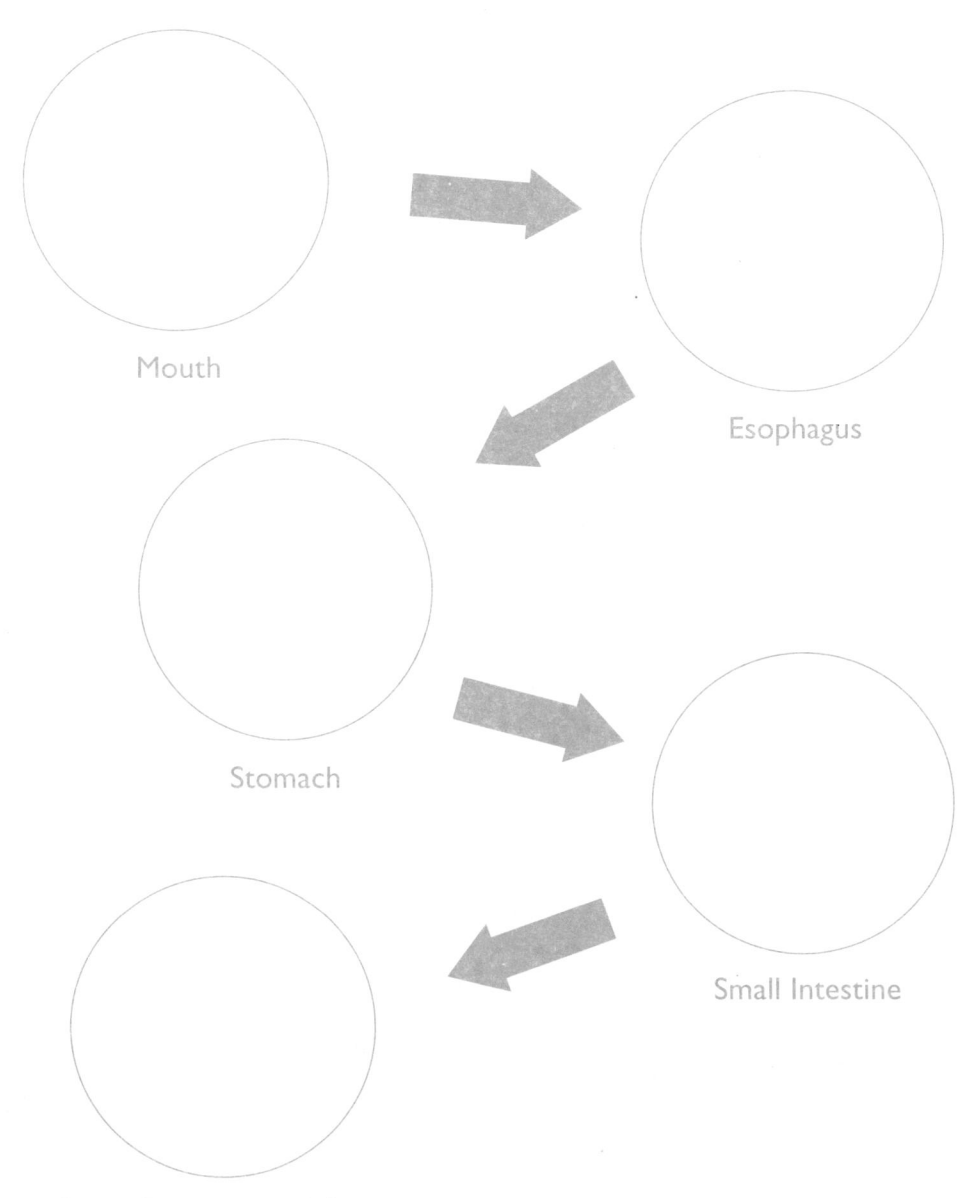

Mouth

Esophagus

Stomach

Small Intestine

Large Intestine and Anus

Each of your digestion stickers shows an everyday activity that resembles the function of an organ in your digestive system. These organs are represented by the circles above. Use the information on the opposite page to help you place each sticker in the correct circle.

Breaking Down a Starch Chain

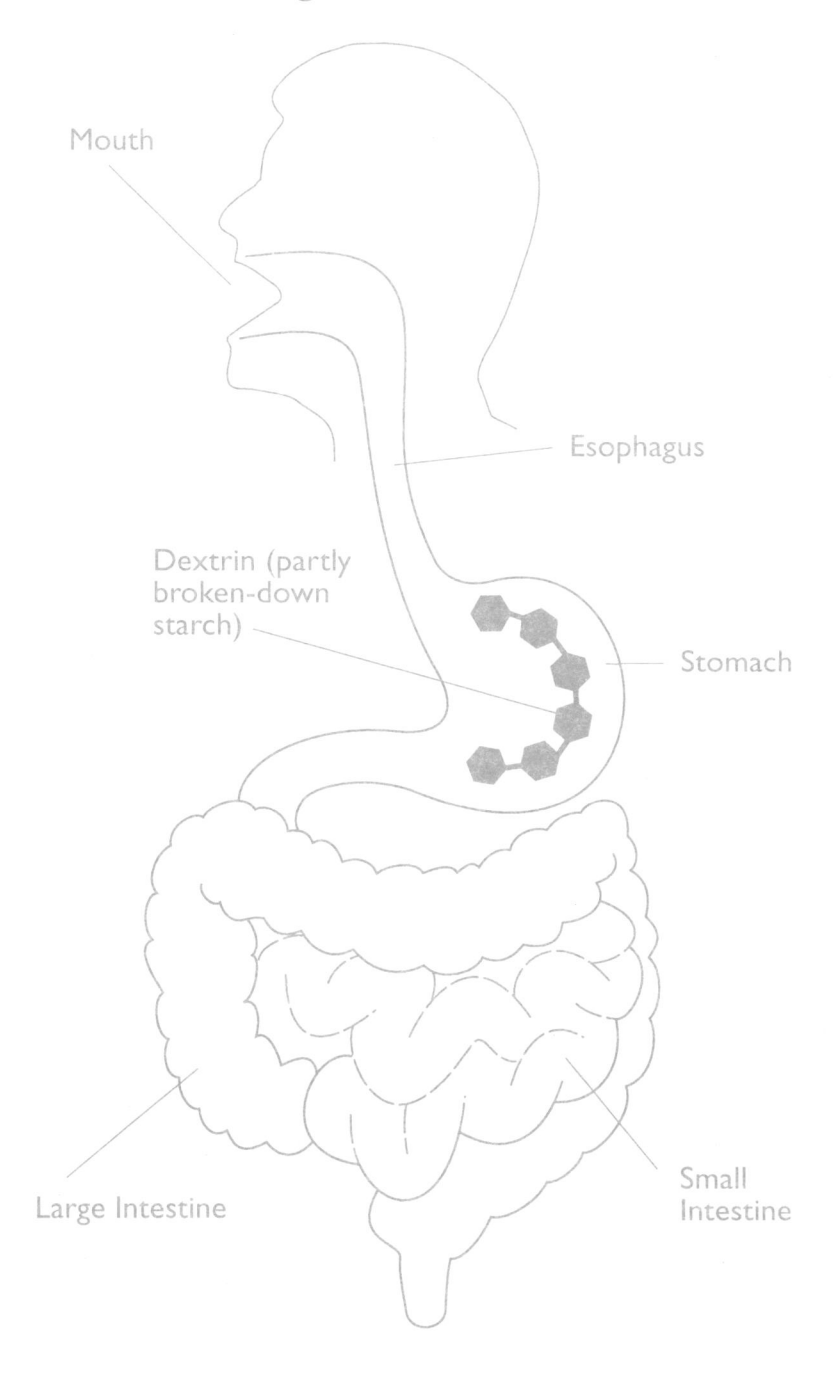

Mouth

Esophagus

Dextrin (partly broken-down starch)

Stomach

Large Intestine

Small Intestine

Use your sugar stickers to create a starch chain, a lactose molecule, and a glucose molecule, and place them in the correct part of the digestive system outlined above. The information on the opposite page will help you.

Make a Dental Record

Baby teeth

Name _____

Baby teeth

Name _____

Adult teeth

Name _____

Adult teeth

Name _____

Above are diagrams of two sets of baby teeth, and two sets of adult teeth. Make a dental record for you and your family by marking each tooth that both you and the diagram have with a cross.
Mark any teeth that the diagram has but you haven't with a diagonal line.

Design a Healthy Daily Diet

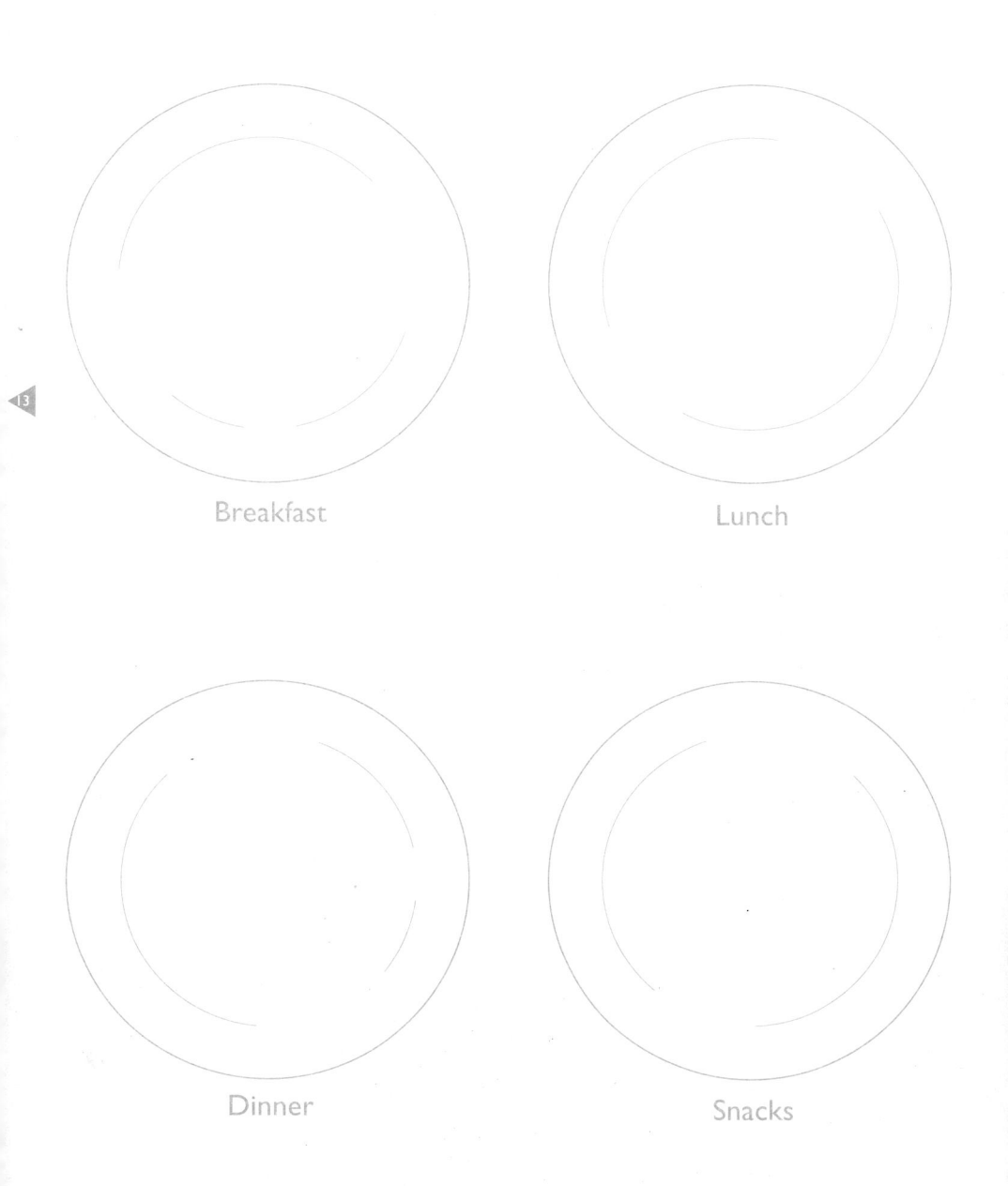

Breakfast

Lunch

Dinner

Snacks

Plan three healthy meals and snacks for a day, using the food pyramid on the opposite page to help you. Draw the meals you plan on the plates above. Does your daily menu contain plenty of carbohydrate and smaller amounts of fat?

How a Kidney Works

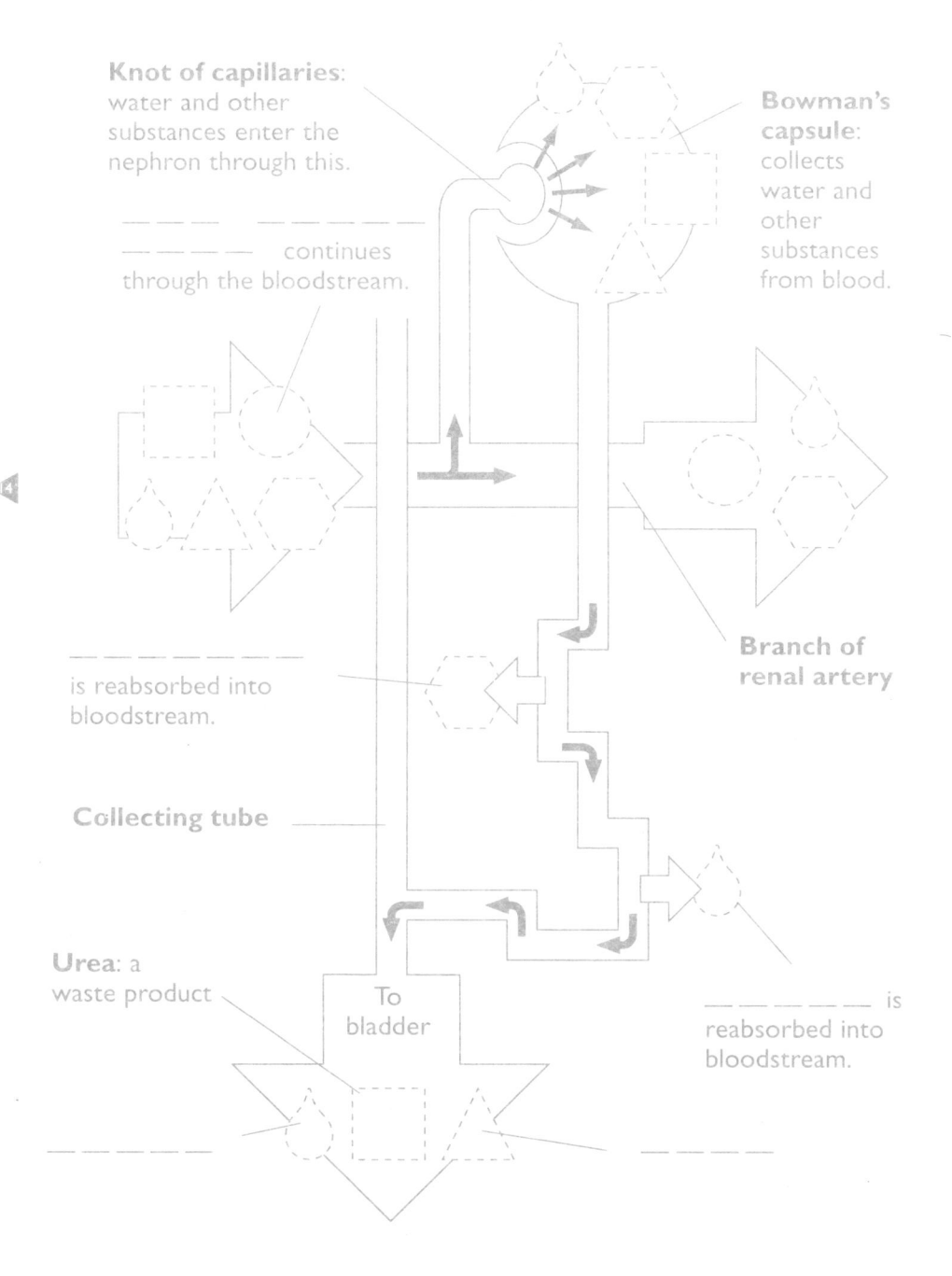

Knot of capillaries: water and other substances enter the nephron through this.

_ _ _ _ _ _ continues through the bloodstream.

Bowman's capsule: collects water and other substances from blood.

Branch of renal artery

_ _ _ _ _ _ is reabsorbed into bloodstream.

Collecting tube

Urea: a waste product

To bladder

_ _ _ _ _ _ is reabsorbed into bloodstream.

The drawing above is a simplified diagram of a nephron. Place your urinary stickers in the correct position on the diagram to see how your kidneys filter waste from your bloodstream. Then complete the missing labels.

Record Your Water Intake

The average daily intake of water by children is 1½ pints. This equals three 8-ounce glasses of water, or six 4-ounce glasses of water. Now let's see how much you drink. Here is a weekly chart.

Quarter pint units

Monday												
Tuesday												
Wednesday												
Thursday												
Friday												
Saturday												
Sunday												

Total amount of water drunk during the week _____ pints.

Your average daily intake (divide total by 7) _____ pints.

Use the chart above to record how much water you drink during a week. Color in a "square" each time you drink one unit, or a ¼ pint (4 oz), of water or watery drink. (A can of cola holds about a ½ pint.) Then fill the totals above to compare your intake with the average intake for a child.

Hormone Sticker Activity

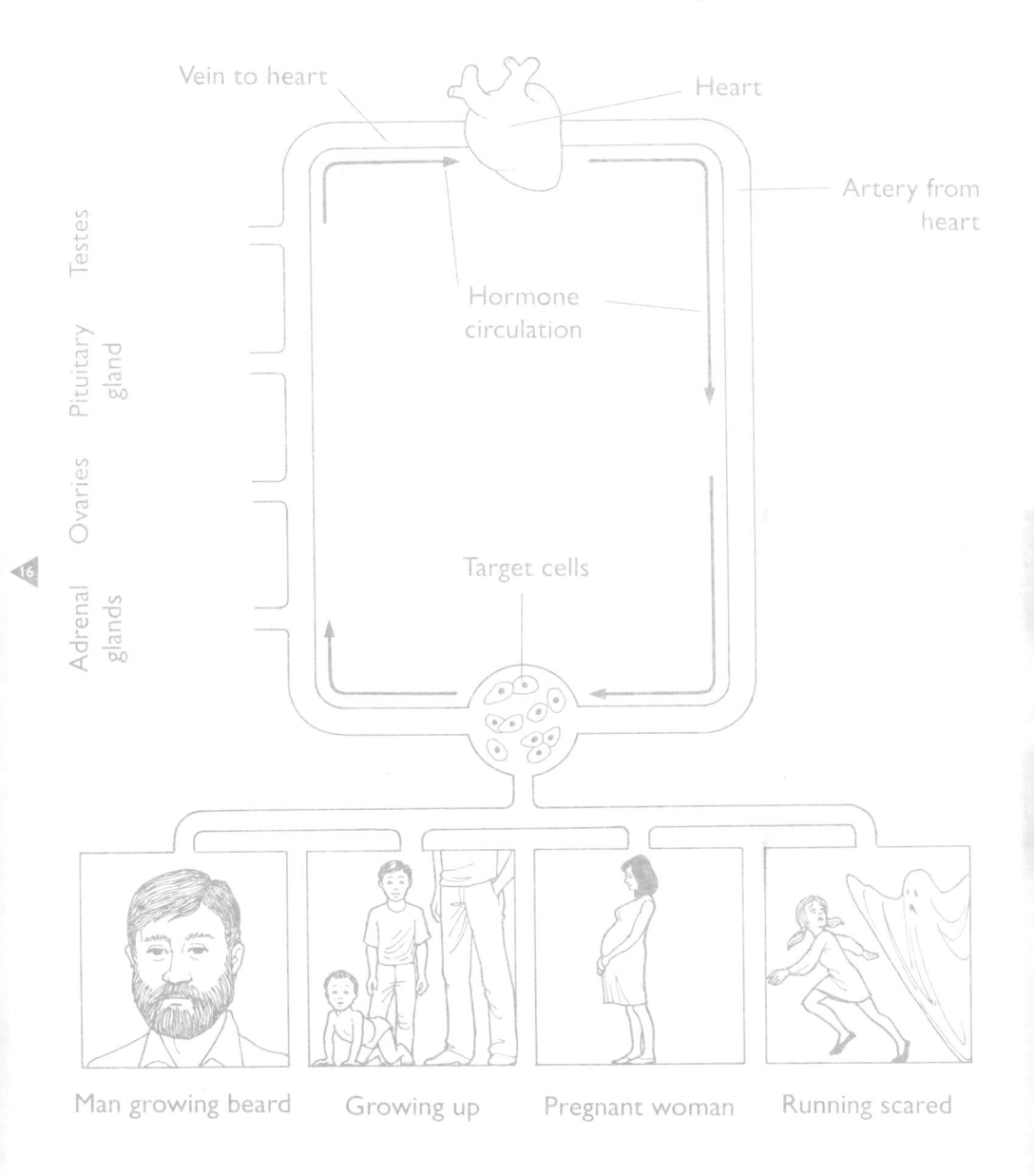

Vein to heart

Heart

Artery from heart

Testes

Pituitary gland

Ovaries

Adrenal glands

Hormone circulation

Target cells

Man growing beard　　Growing up　　Pregnant woman　　Running scared

This simple diagram shows the endocrine system at work. Each picture shows a situation associated with a particular hormone. Place your gland stickers in the correct position on the diagram. Then match each gland to an appropriate picture by drawing a line from the gland, along the vein, through the heart, and along the artery to the matching picture. Use a different color for each line.

An Experiment Using Your Magnifier

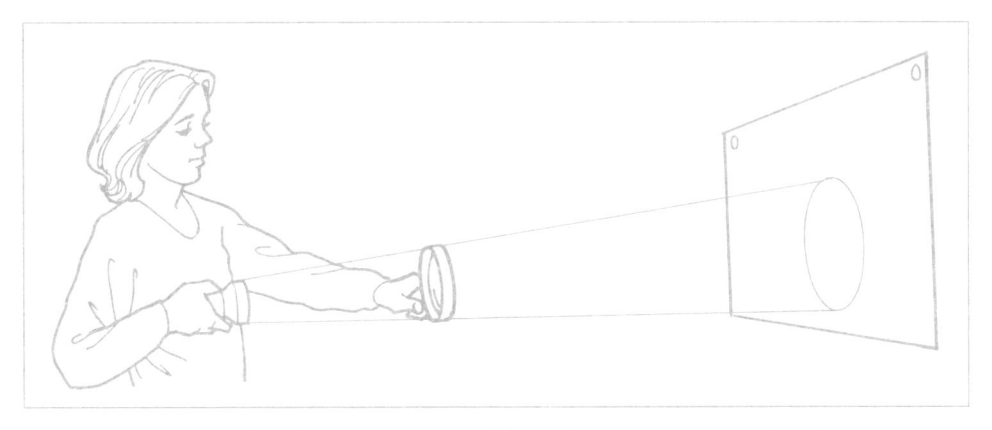

1. Take the magnifier from your tray. Close the drapes to make the room dark. Shine a small, bright flashlight through the magnifier and onto a plain, light wall. Or stick a piece of white paper on the wall.

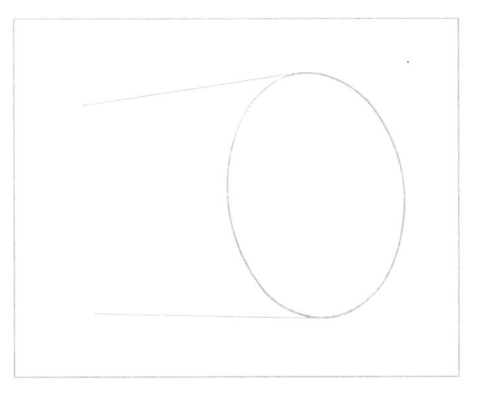

2. Move the magnifier backwards and forwards until the circle of light on the wall has a sharp, clear edge.

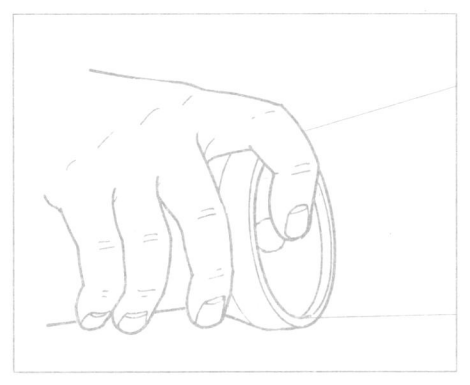

3. Put a finger from the hand holding the flashlight above the bulb, so the finger is in the beam of light.

Look at the image of your finger on the wall. What do you notice about it? _____

A magnifier, like the one in your tray, can bend and focus light rays just like the lens in your eye. You can prove this by following the easy step-by-step instructions for this simple experiment. Then answer the question above.

Making an Ear Trumpet

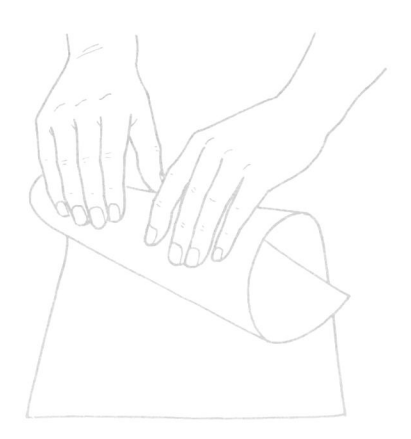

1. Roll a large sheet of paper into a cone.

2. Tape the long edge down.

3. Speak to a friend across the room. Then speak to the friend again, using the cone as a megaphone. What do they notice?

4. Listen to a quiet sound, like a clock ticking. Then use the cone as an ear trumpet by putting it against *but not in* your ear, and listen again.

a) When you use a megaphone, your voice sounds _____

b) When you use an ear trumpet, the sound becomes _____

c) Why does using an ear trumpet have this effect? _____

Follow these easy step-by-step instructions to find out how a simple cone can affect sound waves. Then answer the questions above.

Test Your Senses of Smell and Taste

	Potato	Carrot	Apple
1. Ask an adult to cut some raw potato, carrot, and apple into small bite-size pieces. *Do not do this yourself.*			
2. Blindfold a friend and ask her to taste a piece of each food.	a	b	c
3. Hold your friend's nose, and ask her to taste each piece again.	d	e	f
4. Repeat step 2, but hold a piece of onion under her nose.	g	h	i
	What do the results of your taste test tell you about your sense of taste and smell? _____		

Try these taste tests with a friend. After each taste, ask your friend to guess what she was eating, and write her answer in the box. For example, if she tastes potato while holding her nose, but thinks it is apple, write "apple" in box d.

Test Your Tastebuds

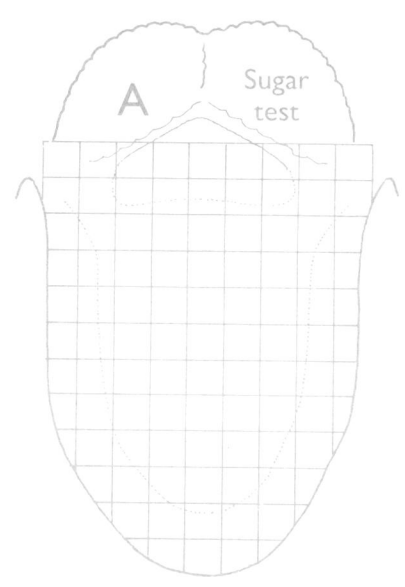

A — Sugar test

B — Orange-peel test

1. Mix a teaspoon of sugar with a little warm water. Blindfold a friend and ask him to stick out his tongue.

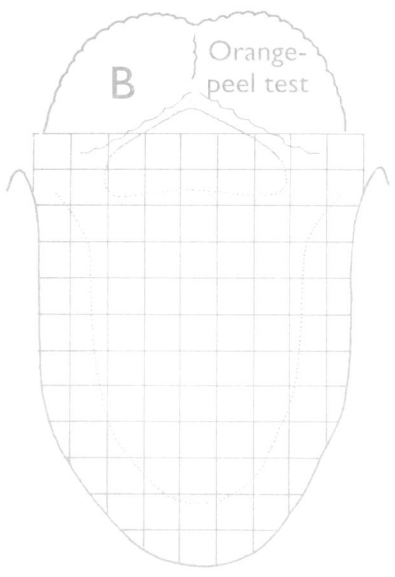

2. Put drops of the sugar mixture on different parts of his or her tongue with a clean spoon.

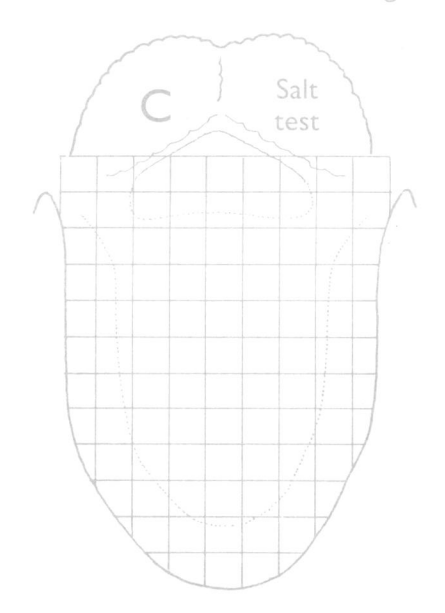

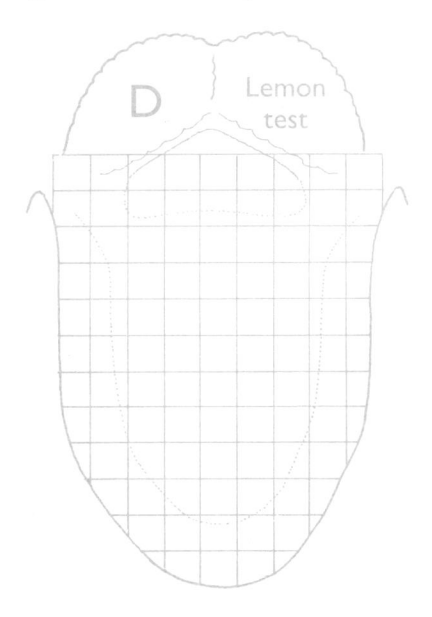

C — Salt test

D — Lemon test

Carry out this test with a friend. Color in red each square on tongue A that matches where your friend can taste sugar most strongly. Repeat the test, using a piece of orange peel. Plot the results on tongue B in blue. Repeat the test with salty water. Plot the results on tongue C in green. Repeat the test using lemon juice. Plot the results on tongue D in yellow. *Do not test any other substances.*

See How a Baby Grows

An egg cell being fertilized by a sperm cell (see page 2).

The developing baby, or fetus, at 5 weeks. Arm and leg buds begin to appear.

The fetus at 8 weeks. One and a quarter inches long. Eyes, ears, mouth, arms, legs, and toes now formed.

The fetus at 12 weeks. Nearly 4 inches long. All internal organs formed.

The fetus at 16 weeks. Five and a half inches long. Face looks human. Blinking and sucking of lips occur.

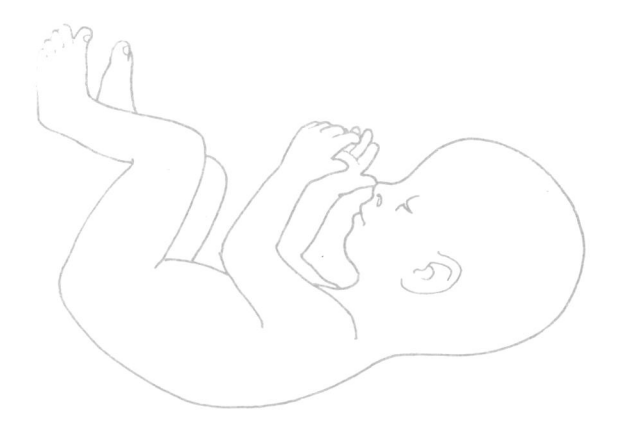

The fetus at 20 weeks. Seven and a half inches long. Hair grows on head and body. Mother can feel baby kicking and hiccuping.

Place your baby stickers in the correct positions above, using the captions as clues. See how much a baby develops in just 20 weeks!

Comparing Family Likenesses

Name	Left handed	Right handed	Height (tall, short, average)	Eye color	Hair color
Mom	✓		short	blue	fair
Most common types					

1. List the names of your grandparents, parents, brothers and sisters down the left-hand column of the grid.

2. At the top of the grid are a series of questions about types of human characteristics. Consider these questions for each member of your family that you have listed.

3. Answer each question by putting a check, size, or color in the correct boxes next to the person's name.

6. Record your family's most common characteristics in the bottom boxes. So, if more of your family have blue eyes than another color, write blue in the last box in the "eye color" column.

Complete this chart by following the simple instructions set out above to discover how alike you and other members of your family are. We have completed the details of an imaginary family member as an example.

Make a Height Chart

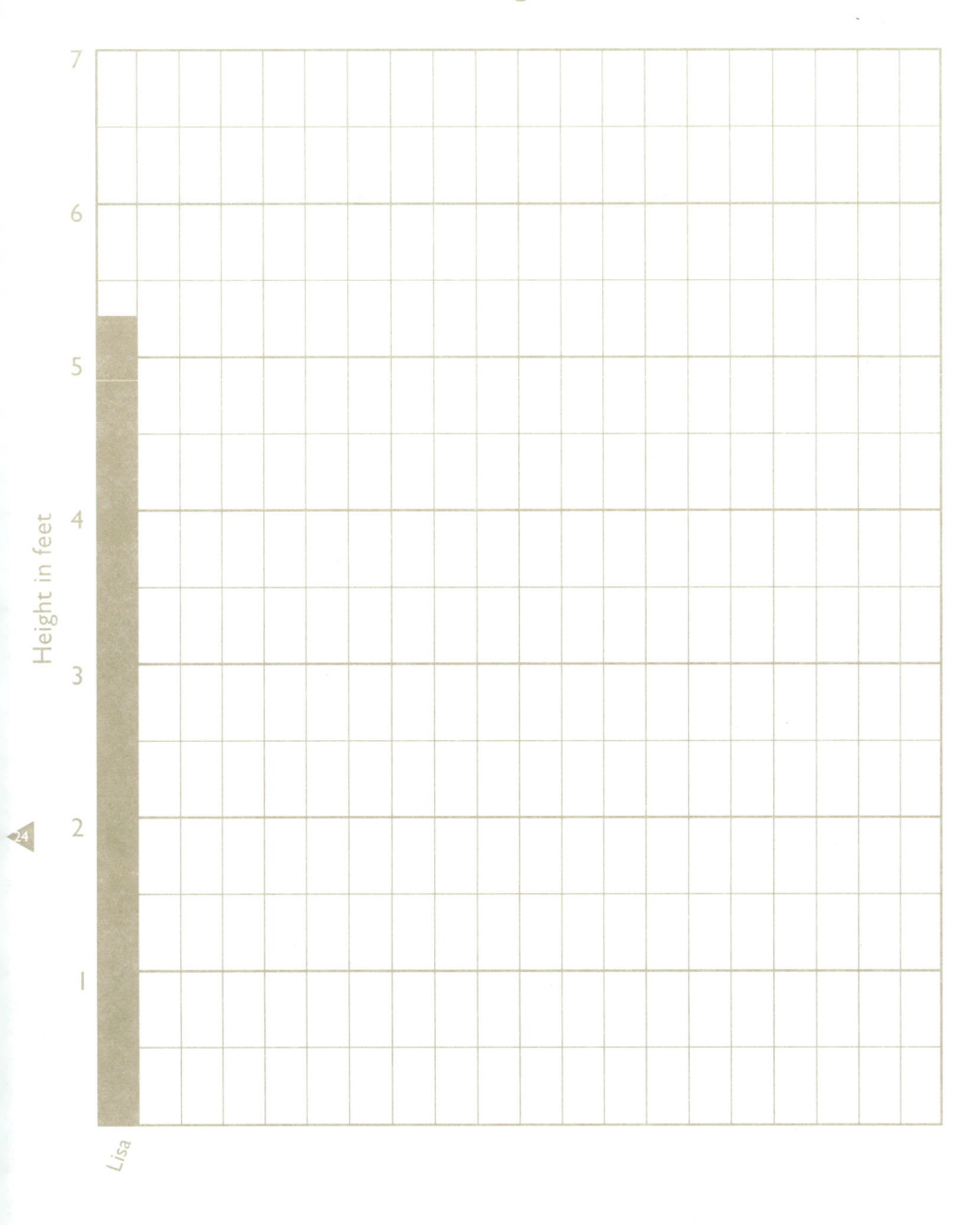

Height in feet

7
6
5
4
3
2
1

Lisa

Make a chart recording how tall you and your classmates are.
To show you how to make the chart,
we have shown the height of an imaginary child, called Lisa,
who is 5 feet 3 inches tall.

Which Muscle?

Follow each of the activities shown below. Can you feel some of your muscles taking the strain. For each activity, circle the muscles being used and name them using the diagram opposite for clues.

1. Bend forward with feet flat on floor.

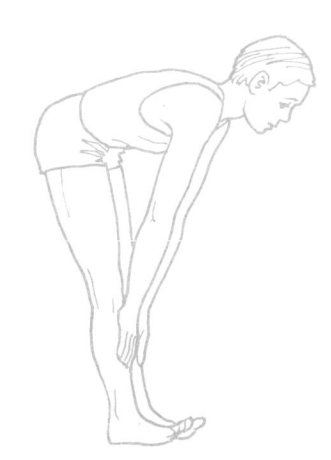

2. Bend forward and raise toes.

3. Hold a heavy book and lift arm.

4. Hold heavy book and lower arm.

5. Crouch down by bending knees.

Voluntary and Involuntary Muscles

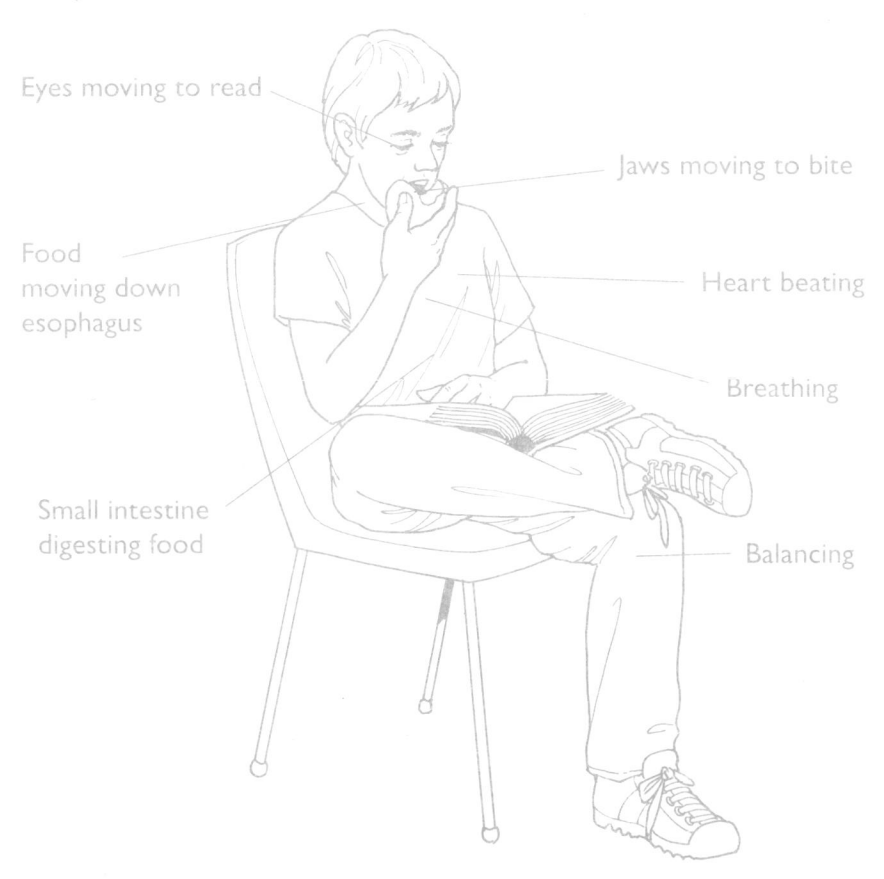

- Eyes moving to read
- Jaws moving to bite
- Food moving down esophagus
- Heart beating
- Breathing
- Small intestine digesting food
- Balancing

Activity	Voluntary muscles	Involuntary muscles
Reading	✓	
Eating		
Swallowing		
Digesting		
Heart		
Breathing		
Balancing		

The boy in this picture is using both voluntary and involuntary muscles. Fill in the chart above to show which type of muscle is powering which activity or bodily function. The first line of the chart has been filled in for you.

Make a Model Rib Cage

B

1. Cut out these shapes and fold along all the dotted lines.

2. Glue the center of the rib cage to section A of the long strip. Make sure you match the two curved shapes.

A

3. Glue tab B of the long strip to the underside of the opposite end.

4. Dab a little glue on the underside of the tabs at the end of each rib. Then stick each tab on top of its matching number on the oval strip.

Xerox this page to twice the size. Use the outlines on the enlarged copy to make a model of a rib cage by following these step-by-step instructions. Can you see how it forms a protective shell for your vital organs?

Flexible Hands

1. Color all the hinge joints in green.

2. Color the sliding joints in red.

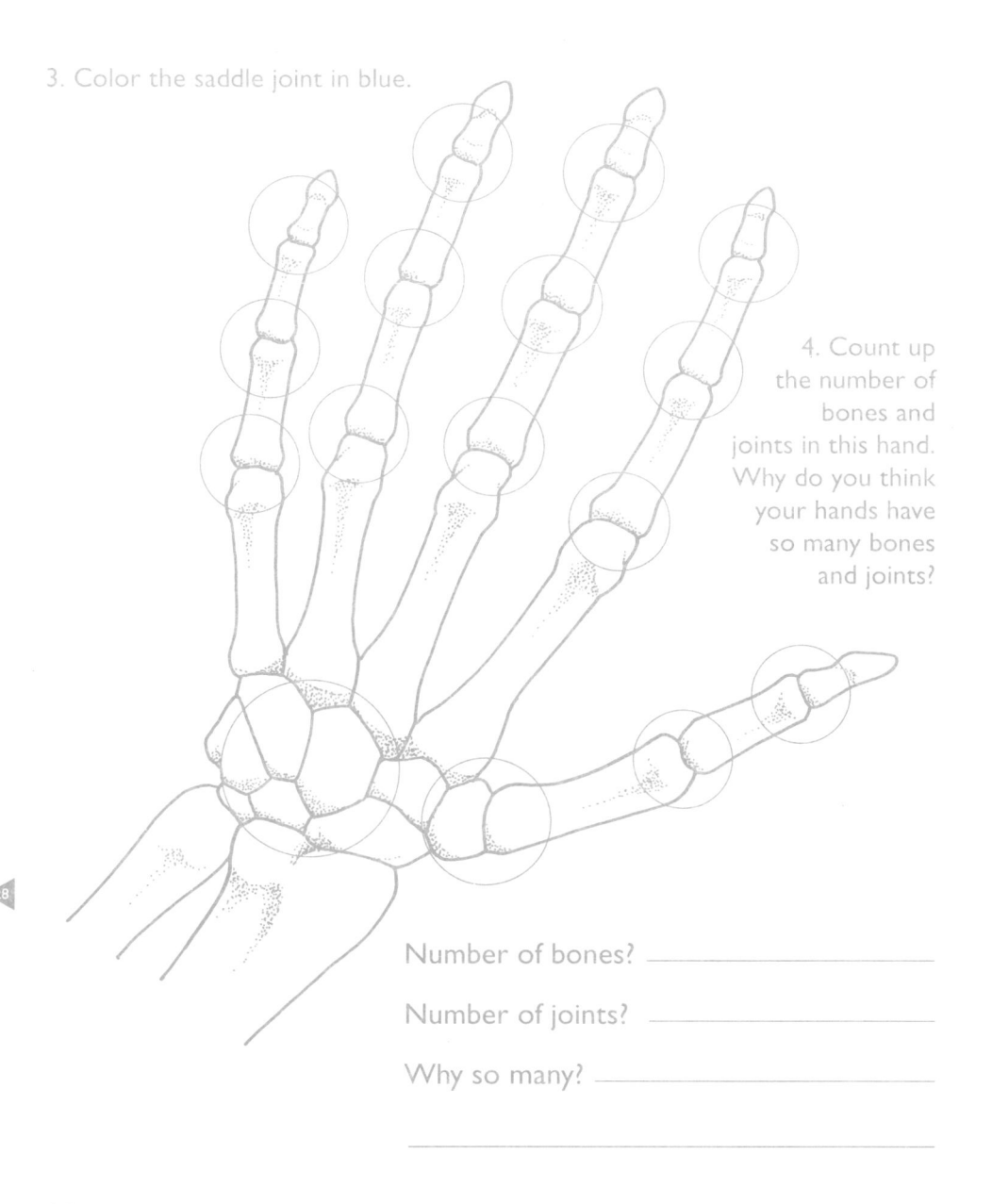

3. Color the saddle joint in blue.

4. Count up the number of bones and joints in this hand. Why do you think your hands have so many bones and joints?

Number of bones? _____

Number of joints? _____

Why so many? _____

_____

The main joints in the hand above have been circled. Color in the circles using the color codes described above. The information on the opposite page will help you, but also test these joints in your own hand to find out how they move.

Making a Paper Bone

A

1. Trace rectangle A onto plain white paper. Cut out the shape, and stick the short edges together to form a cylinder. Repeat this step, so that you have two identical cylinders.

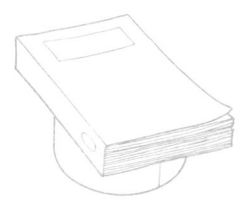

2. Test the strength of one of the cylinders by placing some paperback books on it, one at a time, until the cylinder crumples?

How many books did it take? _____

B

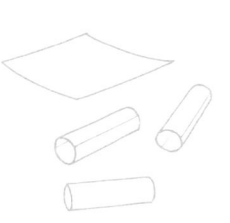

3. Trace rectangles B onto plain paper. Cut out the shapes, and stick together the edges of each to create three small tubes.

4. Pack the small tubes into the second cylinder until it is full. Keep repeating step 3 until you have enough small tubes.

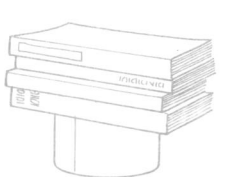

5. Pile some paperback books on top of this cylinder until it crumples.

How many books did it take? _____

Follow these instructions to create a cylinder structured like one of your bones, and discover how strong that structure can be!

Taking Thumb Prints

Name	Name	Name
Pattern	Pattern	Pattern
Name	Name	Name
Pattern	Pattern	Pattern
Name	Name	Name
Pattern	Pattern	Pattern

1. Put a little black ink on the underside of your left thumb. Make a print of it in one of the boxes above by rocking it gently from side to side. Write your name above the print.

2. Examine your print with the magnifier to see which of the basic patterns shown on the opposite page it belongs to. Write the name of the pattern underneath the print.

3. Take thumbprints from your family and friends and record them in the remaining boxes. Which is the most common type of pattern amongst your family and friends?

The most common basic pattern recorded was _____

Use this chart to record your thumbprint and those of your family and friends.

Make a Hair Chart

15									
14									
13									
12									
11									
10									
9									
8									
7									
6									
5									
4									
3									
2									
1	■								
	Dark	Fair	Blonde	Dark	Fair	Blonde	Dark	Fair	Blonde
	Wavy			Curly			Straight		

Count up how many pupils in your class have wavy hair, how many have straight hair, and how many have curly hair. Fill in this chart by filling in one square for each pupil. We have started the chart for you by recording the details of an imaginary pupil with dark, wavy hair.

ANSWERS

PAGE 2

1. Draw a nerve cell
2. Draw an intestinal cell
3. Draw a sperm cell
4. Draw an egg cell

PAGE 4

Position of body organs (clockwise, starting top right):

Brain

Heart

Left lung

Left kidney

Stomach

Right kidney

Liver

Right lung

PAGE 6

Picture A should be easier to remember because it has a "regular" pattern

PAGE 7

1. Reflex
2. Non-reflex
3. Reflex
4. Reflex
5. Reflex
6. Non-reflex
7. Non-reflex
8. Non-reflex

PAGE 8

Candle went out first in Jar A

The main gas in Jar A after you have breathed into it is carbon dioxide (CO_2)

PAGE 10

Mouth – Cutting action

Esophagus – Squeezing toothpaste

Stomach – Food mixer

Small intestine – Absorbent sponge

Large Intestine and Anus – Emptying trash

PAGE 11

The long starch chain goes in the mouth and esophagus.

Two-sugar molecules go in the top part of the small intestine.

Single-sugar molecules go in the bottom part of the small intestine.

PAGE 14

Position of urinary stickers, (clockwise, starting top left):

Red blood cell

Water

Salt

Water

Glucose

PAGE 16

Running scared – Adrenal gland

Pregnant woman – Ovaries

Growing up – Pituitary gland

Man growing beard – Testes

PAGE 17

The image of your finger should be upside down.

PAGE 18

a) Louder

b) Louder

c) Because the ear trumpet channels sound waves into your ear.

PAGE 25

1. Quadriceps femoris
2. Quadriceps femoris and gastrocnemius
3. Biceps
4. triceps
5. Hamstring

PAGE 26

Eating
 = Voluntary

Swallowing
 = Involuntary

Digesting
 = Involuntary

Heart
 = Involuntary

Breathing
 = Involuntary

Balancing
 = Voluntary

PAGE 28

Sliding joints (color red) – the bones in your wrist.

Saddle joint (color blue) – at base of thumb.

Hinge joints (color green) – all the other bones in fingers and thumb.

There are 27 bones in each hand.

Your hands have a large number of bones to give them great dexterity (ability to move in many directions).